PIONEERING
SPIRIT

An Anglo-Argentine Story of My Ancestors, My Mother and Me

*healing the
ancestral timeline*

JEANINE BROWNRIGG

BALBOA.PRESS
A DIVISION OF HAY HOUSE

with love and thanks for
your contribution. x

Balboa Press books may be ordered through booksellers or by contacting:

Balboa Press
A Division of Hay House
1663 Liberty Drive
Bloomington, IN 47403
www.balboapress.co.uk
UK TFN: 0800 0148647 (Toll Free inside the UK)
UK Local: 02036 956325 (+44 20 3695 6325 from outside the UK)

Because of the dynamic nature of the Internet, any web addresses or links contained in this book may have changed since publication and may no longer be valid. The views expressed in this work are solely those of the author and do not necessarily reflect the views of the publisher, and the publisher hereby disclaims any responsibility for them.

The author of this book does not dispense medical advice or prescribe the use of any technique as a form of treatment for physical, emotional, or medical problems without the advice of a physician, either directly or indirectly. The intent of the author is only to offer information of a general nature to help you in your quest for emotional and spiritual well-being. In the event you use any of the information in this book for yourself, which is your constitutional right, the author and the publisher assume no responsibility for your actions.

Any people depicted in stock imagery provided by Getty Images are models, and such images are being used for illustrative purposes only. Certain stock imagery © Getty Images.

Print information available on the last page.

ISBN: 978-1-9822-8238-7 (sc)
ISBN: 978-1-9822-8239-4 (e)

Balboa Press rev. date: 12/17/2020

DEDICATION

To Mum

for without you, this book would never have been written

and

to my Ancestors

for without you, I would have no story to tell.

CONTENTS

PART 3

ME

PREFACE

Pioneering Spirit tells the story of my ancestors, my mother and me, inspired by my mother when she asked me to write her memoir. She always said she had enough stories to fill a book and, indeed she had lived a rich and varied life up to her passing in her 90th year. She was born in England, lived half her life in Argentina, crisscrossing the Atlantic Ocean more times that she could remember, before finally returning to live in the land of her birth when she was 40 years old. She was raised in privileged circumstances; experienced the war years as a volunteer; struggled to make a living; and in the last 20 years of her life became a respected and internationally renowned healer.

I loved her deeply and had always enjoyed listening to her stories but I didn't take her request seriously, unwilling to take on board the task she wished to place on my shoulders, even though she kept saying I was the writer in the family and clearly she had faith I could do justice to her request. I admit to have enjoyed writing since I was young, mostly letters to family and friends. Twenty years ago I had a holiday in Egypt cruising down the Nile and visiting the tombs and temples of its ancient past. The experience captivated my creative spirit and my writing took a dive into a different level as I wrote about all I had seen. After that I began a daily journal, finding that by offloading my deepest thoughts and feelings I could make sense of what was going on in my life, which at the time seemed to be spiralling out of control. My journal became my solace, my inner world became my sanctuary and writing was the way to take me there.

Writing letters to friends and family and private journaling is one thing, but I had not thought of myself as an author and sharing my writing in the world. However, life has a habit of taking you where you least want to go. As my mother neared the end of her life, her stories became more vivid and emotional and I found my resolve softening until I reached the point of knowing I would undertake the task she left me. The seed had been sown. It had merely needed time to germinate and grow.

At the end of 2008, I began making notes of her stories and writing these down while on holiday in Argentina, the country where it had all begun; where I was born and where my mother had always called home. On returning to England in March 2009, I typed up my notes to create an outline of her life. I had the information, yet I knew I wanted to find a way to go deeper to do credit to the woman who had been at the centre of my life and who had achieved so much. I felt compelled to write continuously for three months until on 18th June, she passed away. It was as though I had needed to write as much as I could before she made her transition.

I put my writing to one side as my brother, David, and I focused on clearing her house and letting go of her earthly possessions. Mum had always found it hard to throw anything away and every room was filled to the brim, including a vast library of more than 800 books. It took us almost nine months to complete and left us mentally, physically and emotionally exhausted and vowing not to leave the same task to our children. Her house was sold and it was time to say goodbye to her earthly home. I walked through each room for one last time sensing her presence, thanking her and her house for all the happy times we had shared together. I closed the door and walked away.

Grief is a process, which cannot be hurried and it was another four years before I began writing again. For the first time in many years, my husband and I were not going to Argentina to enjoy the summer sunshine and I found writing an escape during the cold, dark English winter. The intervening years had helped me to let go of the initial sadness and sense of loss at my mother's passing and I felt more at peace when I returned to my notes. I went through the papers and photograph albums I had kept, finding letters and documents among her possessions, which gave me further insights into her life and provided the basis of my memories of her and the stories she told. It was these that started a journey for me to look back in time at when and where her story really began.

As I reviewed my mother's life, I began to notice the similarity of my own experiences. I had likewise been born in one country and spent my life in another, as had my father and both my maternal and paternal grandparents. Was it possible that the choices my parents and ancestors had made generations before had influenced my life? I had never thought about this before. As far as I was concerned, my life had unfolded because of the choices I had made, apart from those my parents had made for me as a child. I began to reflect on my life and slowly a bigger picture emerged as I realised I wanted to expand the scope of my mother's request and include our family story, as well as my own journey, through my ancestors. As I connected to my past, I identified patterns that had been passed down the family line, which helped me to understand the ancestral inheritance of leaving our homelands and the separation from loved ones throughout the generations.

My mother inspired, guided and helped me find my way in the world during her life and since her death continues to do so. Through the writing of this book, I have taken a journey, which has been challenging and deeply rewarding. I am grateful to her for the opportunity it has given me to learn more about myself that I never would have discovered if I had not undertaken the task she entrusted to me, as well as connecting with my conscious creative spirit that otherwise would never have found a voice.

Jeanine Brownrigg
November 2020

ACKNOWLEDGEMENTS

I would like to send my deepest heartfelt thanks to all those people who appeared in my life as if by magic to help and support me in writing this book.

With special thanks to:

Julia McCutchen, Founder and Creative Director of the International Association for Conscious and Creative Writers and Conscious Writing, Living and Leadership, who gave me the opportunity to access my authentic voice as a conscious creative writer.

The Susan Mears Literary Agency who acted as my agent from 2017-2020 and introduced me to Wendy Yorke, my Book Editor and Author Coach who believed in me and the message this book brings to its readers. I am grateful to Wendy for her ongoing guidance and support.

Jan Gavin for editing the early drafts of the manuscript.

Natalia O'Sullivan, healer and spiritual counsellor for guiding me to connect with my ancestors.

Isabella Kirton Bourne, Heather MacIver Jewell and Margaret (Miggy) Deyes Sayers and my friends from St Hilda's College, Hurlingham, Argentina for a lifetime of love and friendship.

Ann Brownrigg, in collaboration with the late Henry Brownrigg and Henry Pythian-Adams, in researching the Brownrigg family tree; and Suzanne Paget for connecting me with my ancestors in New Zealand. Also Glascott Symes who guided us on the ancestral trail in Ireland. With their assistance and extensive research, my knowledge of our ancestral story has expanded beyond what I learned from my parents during their lifetime.

The late Peggy James who located the grave of my great aunt Evelyn Hoyle in the Anglican Cemetery in La Cumbre, Argentina.

Richard and Caroline Leach in Jujuy, friends in Buenos Aires, Hurlingham, La Cumbre in Argentina and Punta del Este in Uruguay who opened up their hearts and homes to us on our trips to the southern hemisphere.

My mother's Touch for Health friends and colleagues who helped me unravel her healer's journey and have shared their thoughts about her healing work.

My husband, for taking me back to Argentina and putting up with my endless hours at my computer.

And my family, who share in this story as much I do.

To all those people who have been part of my conscious writing journey, my readers and friends, you have my deepest gratitude and appreciation.

I also wish to thank the families of the late Margaret Sayers and Jacky McBroome who have given permission for their contributions to be included after their loved ones sadly passed away during the publication of my book.

"At first glance this book might appear to be just another autobiography. However, it is in fact a profound broadening of the concept itself and may herald a ground-breaking change to how future authors should approach the genre.

"Jeanine Brownrigg begins this "pioneering" work with a biographical account of her family's ancestral roots and her mother's later-in-life passion for helping and healing others. Part 3, the autobiographical section, is where Jeanine, through the cathartic experience of the writing process, draws together and exposes the deep layers of psychological structuring and emotional trauma involved in her personal manifestation of Joseph Campbell's "hero's journey."

"She reaches an understanding rather than the ever-elusory end to this journey. That is, that we are each a unique representation of a multi-layered, multi-dimensional expression of Consciousness (or God, if you prefer). By exploring and healing our ancestral timelines together with our spiritual lifetimes, we become more able to fully express our personality in the present.

"Pioneering Spirit provides a vital step in the understanding of our 'Self' and the many psychological and emotional influences that govern our automatic ways of thinking, believing, and behaving. We are experiencing a great "awakening" in humanity's perception of reality. Our individual awakening requires us to identify those core archetypal beliefs within us that unconsciously stymie the fullest expression of who we are and why we are here at this momentous time in our evolution."

Chris W.E. Johnson MSc—Author of It's About You! Know Your Self. Member of the Scientific and Medical Network.

"This book is a beautiful account of bravery and courage in the face of adversity lived out across the generations. It is a humbling tale of love across the oceans and of two very different countries. A look back on the history of the world, of humans carving out their marks and those people whose lives have become the legacy for the next generations, uncovering more stories and mysteries, and unwittingly holding the keys to their own healing. This book brilliantly reveals the unfolding of an ancestry through the tales of pioneering spirits whether for love or necessity, witnessing how everything, eventually, comes together; the synchronicities; the change of beliefs about oneself and about the world; but most importantly, the belief in oneself to come out victorious, despite all odds; and the wisdom that stems from it all. In the space of a few hours, while reading Jeanine Brownrigg's excellent book, Pioneering Spirit, I became someone else. I became the author and I felt her pain, but also her happiness. This is her story and she has certainly found her voice among the sorrow and suffering. I applaud her for speaking up for all of us to hear."

Diane Faoutolo, Writer.

"This book is an inspiring and heartfelt tribute to Joan Brownrigg, lovingly put together by her daughter, to somebody who was and always will be a very important part of my own journey. Jeanine has re-visited so much of what was also part of my childhood, which made reading Joan's story all the more interesting for me personally. There are so many other people who will find her journey just as fascinating. Joan Brownrigg was a role model for me as a child, I loved being in her home; she was the epitome of the perfect mother who provided a loving environment for us children and copious cakes and inspiring games to keep us happy. Meeting her again as an adult was equally wonderful, now she was not only the mother of my dearest childhood friend, but a healer with many strings to her bow. I embraced her convictions and over the ensuing years, benefitted constantly from her teachings and her healings. There never seemed to be any ache or pain, be it physical or spiritual, that she could not shift in some way. I consider myself extremely fortunate to have known Joan and to have been allowed to share so much of her family life as well.

"Jeanine has captured so vividly the steps of her journey but added to it the vast experience that she too has gained from piecing together her ancestry and the realisation that there is an ancestral pattern, which seems to be deeply embedded in our psyche. Her insights and conclusions, reached after many years of following her own healing path, are without doubt going to help many of us who are seeking to understand ourselves better and to eventually come to terms with our own realities, as we move along in our life's journey with acceptance and happiness as our goal."

Heather Van den Broucque, Reiki Practitioner, former Chair Anglo-Argentine Society and David Jewell, business executive.

"This book reminds me how important it is to have courage and know that we all have an important role in life in terms of service to other people, but to also look after our own needs and health. Joan Brownrigg's story of her life and work after her husband's death is particularly poignant for me. Jeanine has a lovely engaging style of writing which flows beautifully to reveal the romantic, poetic and artistic side of her character. She gives us hope and inspiration to follow our calling and find acceptance thorough simply allowing innate gifts and talents to be shared for the good of other people. Despite her losses and grief, Joan established the next chapter of her life and helped so many people. As a mother, widow and fellow healer, I found her story moving and inspirational. Life is not always an easy path to walk and there can be many obstacles, both real and imagined along the way. There is so much suffering in the world, and Joan's story is a timely reminder that we all have important work to do and share. Healing the wound of separation is an inside job with all its twists and turns. Eventually we may realise that love is the true answer to all our problems and woes and Life is taking us home. Through this book, Jeanine and her mother's story help us to realise that home is truly where the heart is and that transformation is possible."

Tracy Gibbons @tracyanngibbons
Wellbeing Therapist

"Reading this book gave me a terrific boost in my efforts to beat anxiety. Through the retelling of her family story, the author has given me more confidence that healing is possible and that it comes from within. There is an inspirational tone to the book, particularly the final chapters as all the strands come together. I highly recommend this book to people who are interested in people and are open minded about the possibilities of life. I think readers will quickly be hooked in, particularly when they understand how the book operates on two levels: a family memoir; and a look at universal issues. They will also like the easy, intelligent, unpretentious written style."

John Robinson, retired College Principal.

"Pioneering Spirit is a real inspiration. By delving into the past the author has created her own "Who do you think you are?" Reading Jeanine Brownrigg's book inspired me to research my own family background. I know nothing about my maternal grandfather, except that he was born in Sheffield and went to Argentina around 1910. I also feel motivated to write my own memories, leaving something for my grandsons to read about their ancestors when they are older. My own mother died when I was 22 and I never really found anything out about her war years; like Jeanine's parents she volunteered in the World War Two effort. I will highly recommend this book to my family, friends and colleagues because it gives such a wonderful insight into how courageous our ancestors were to leave the country of their birth and travel into the unknown. In those days they were presented with so many challenges.

"Not only does this book fulfil her mother's wishes of writing about her amazing life, but the author also shares her own transformational, healing journey. I have had the privilege of being in both their lives since I was about five years old, living very close to them in Hurlingham, Argentina. Joan Brownrigg was my mentor, surrogate mother and friend. I was lucky enough to experience Joan's unique healing methods many times, even from afar. On one occasion I was in Cordoba City, Argentina and had a horrendous sore throat. I rang Joan from a public phone and in no time at all she had 'tuned in' and hey presto, the sore throat disappeared!

"Jeanine Brownrigg explains that writing this book has given her the opportunity to find her voice. She has blossomed like a beautiful flower, starting with her petals closed in a very tight bud, the flower has emerged into a beautiful specimen. There were times when I saw Jeanine so full of sadness. However, after all those wonderful summers spent in the southern hemisphere, she started to emerge and is now a different person. Through this book, she shares her emotions and has become a wonderful healer in her own right. This book really moved me. I felt the great contrasts of emotions the author has managed to convey. Bringing together her mother's inspirational story and the sadness Joan experienced in not wanting to return to Argentina, and the author's own journeys to Argentina which helped her heal her sadness. After reading the last chapter I felt a huge feeling of joy and happiness. Her mother would be very proud of what she has achieved. Congratulations, Jeanine!"
Margaret Sayers, retired Complementary Therapist.

"Pioneering Spirit inspires and educates. Jeanine acquaints us with various holistic therapies significant to her mother and herself. Yet the heart in this tale is her honesty. While exposing the pain and vulnerability that may attend a search to know and heal ourselves she imparts a deep sense of the mystery and synchronicity that guide and accompany us on that journey. Her insights offer hope in those moments when the dark night of the soul descends and the seeker confronts despair. For 'though the way may be uncertain', for those that trust, 'the power of Love' is the ultimate illumination."
Pratibha Castle, Shamanic Heart Reiki Master and writer.

Pratibha's prizewinning poetry pamphlet publishes through Hedgehog Poetry Press. Her work is featured in various journals and anthologies, and a selection of her poems can be read on The Blue Nib, Impressed and Words for the Wild sites.

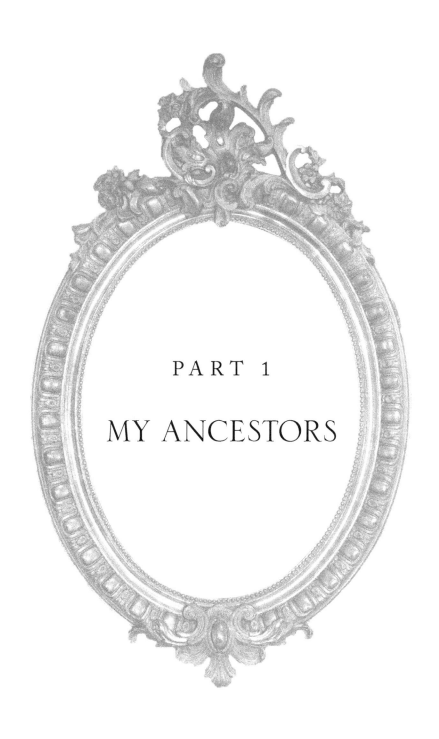

PART 1

MY ANCESTORS

WE ALL HAVE A
STORY TO TELL

We all have a story to tell, who we are, where we come from and where we are going as our lives unfold before us, on our human journey. Our stories are unique and yet each of our individual stories contributes to our global story of humanity as we leave our footprints in the never-ending story of the evolution of Planet Earth. In some ways we are artists painting pictures as our lives unfold before us and, if we can for a moment stand back and observe the overall picture, like an artist does as he or she paints the canvas, we may get to see the perfection of every choice we made, which results in a masterpiece of our own creation.

We may not see the perfection when our lives are filled with despair and suffering as that only comes when we reach a level of understanding that acknowledges the soul's journey through lifetime after lifetime. We are born into a family that can help us heal the past and recreate a new future except we are mostly unaware we carry the unconscious burdens of our ancestors that can make the path difficult at times. But by becoming aware we are merely following in their footsteps, we can make a different choice and go another way.

The world in which we live is very different to that of our ancestors and yet, despite advances in all aspects of our culture, society, scientific and technological achievements over the centuries, humanity continues to face wars, conflicts and natural disasters, which cause people to leave their homelands and move from one country to another for survival in search of a better life. While we may no longer look for new pastures to graze our cattle and fields to grow crops like our ancestors, migration is as much a current global issue now as it has been throughout the history of our planetary evolution.

Pioneering Spirit tells our family story of migration and how our ancestors chose to leave the land of their birth in England, Scotland and Ireland and travel thousands of miles across the globe to establish a new life in New Zealand and Argentina. Whilst our story is unique it does share a common theme of those who continue to travel the world to earn a living in order to have a better life than their country of origin can offer. This pattern passes down the generations and it may be that your family shares a similar story. *Pioneering Spirit* is not only a family story but also takes a deeper look into the emotional trauma that affects the generations and how it is possible to heal the wounds of the past and free us up for a happier, healthier life. It is a story of transformation and change and maybe can inspire you to reflect on your ancestral lineage and discover treasures that may lie hidden deep within your own unique family story. You never know what you might find, but first you have to be willing and curious to open the door.

CHAPTER 1

PATERNAL

I come from a family of pioneers who chose to leave their homelands and seek their fortune in a new land. The Brownrigg ancestors originated from England in the northern counties of Cumberland and Yorkshire. A Hall of Names research also identified the first record of the name Brownrigg in East Lothian, Scotland, which suggests they moved across the border into England. The earliest ancestor recorded in our family tree is probably Gawen Brownrigg of Holm Cultram, Cumbria in the 1500s. His great great grandson, Gawen, had two sons, George and Henry. Our branch of the family tree descends from the Giles line who was possibly a cousin. It is thought that Giles Brownrigg was born in Crosthwaite, Cumberland about 1640 although no birth record has ever been found. We know that Giles was related to Henry, brother of George, through recent DNA testing results of Ann Brownrigg's son and a member of the Henry line, although the exact relationship is not specified. The George line died out.

Around 1685 Giles Brownrigg decided to migrate to Ireland and settled in St Annagh, near Wingfield, County Wexford, where he probably established himself as a farmer continuing the profession of his family and ancestors. Giles's death is recorded in 1702, aged 62, as a result from a fall from his horse. Many of his descendants were farmers who leased land and released it at a profit. Others migrated overseas to Australia, New Zealand, Canada, South Africa, Argentina, Brazil, and Costa Rica, seeking fortune and adventure and some went into the Church. One of these was my great grandfather, Robert Graham Brownrigg, who was born in County Wexford in 1819, the son of Robert Brownrigg of Norris Mount and Elizabeth Graham. He became a minister in the Church of Ireland and was ordained in 1848. He was appointed the Vicar of Clonagoose between 1851-65 and the Vicar of Barragh between 1865-68. During this time he travelled to England to visit his brother, the Reverend Thomas Richard Brownrigg who was a curate at Steep Church in Petersfield, Hampshire. On one of his visits he met and married Amelia Coker Worthington who was originally from Bath and was living in Portsea Island, Hampshire.

I knew little about my great grandmother, Amelia, when I began to write my story but my daughter's move to Bath prompted me to do more research. I discovered that Amelia Coker Worthington was the second daughter of John and Elizabeth Worthington from Clifton in Bristol. Amelia's mother, Elizabeth was born in 1794 and her father, Charles Worthington was born in 1762, a descendent of an ancient Lancashire family. They had two daughters, Charlotte Mary and Elizabeth. Charles's profession is described as being of Lincoln's Inn, London. Charles and Elizabeth Worthington lived in Lansdown Crescent, a fashionable area in the City of Bath. Their house was built in a similar style to the more famous Royal Crescent, overlooking fields and pasture lands with grazing sheep, offering unparalleled views across the city, which remains so to this day.

Charles Worthington died in 1819, aged 57, leaving his daughters as his heirs. His daughter, Elizabeth, married John Pistor in the Parish of Walcot, Bath on the 25 May 1826. On their marriage, John Pistor adopted the name Worthington by Royal Decree so his wife could inherit. John and Elizabeth lived in Clifton, Bristol. Their second daughter, Amelia, was born in 1830 and baptised in Bath Abbey, as recorded in the Register of Baptisms:

> *'On 20 May 1830 at Bath Abbey, Amelia Coker Worthington,*
> *daughter of John and Elizabeth, of Clifton.'*

The family left Clifton and moved to Bath around 1831, initially living in Lansdown Place East. They later moved to Elizabeth's father's house in Lansdown Crescent. Amelia had six siblings, although baptism records show she was the only child to be baptised in Bath Abbey.

At some point John and Elizabeth left Bath and moved to Portsea Island in Hampshire, establishing their new home at Kent House in Southsea. It was here that John Worthington died in January 1854. The following year, on 10 April 1855, Amelia married the Reverend Robert Graham Brownrigg at St Jude's Church in Southsea. The ceremony was officiated by Robert's brother, Reverend Thomas Richard Brownrigg who had become the first incumbent at St Jude's. Their marriage was recorded in the Norfolk Chronicle dated 21 April 1855:

> *'On the 10th, at Southsea, the Rev. Robt. G. Brownrigg, Vicar*
> *of Clonagoose, County Carlow, to Amelia Coker, second*
> *daughter of the late John W, Esq. of Kent House, Southsea,*
> *and formerly of Lansdown Crescent, Bath.'*
> *(source: www.genesreunited.co.uk).*

Thus it was that Amelia left the land of her birth and moved to Ireland with her new husband and settled into being the wife of a minister. They had five children and their sixth child and second son, Gerald Worthington, was born, on 11 January 1867, who was to become my grandfather. At the time Robert Graham was Vicar of Barragh, in Newtownberry, Enniscorthy in the County of Wexford. Robert Graham and his family continued to live in the area and serve the parishes of Kilrush 1868-75; Fethard 1875-77; and Crosspatrick and Kilcommon 1877-85 until he retired and moved with his family to Dundrum, a suburb of Dublin. Robert Graham died in

1891, aged 79. Amelia died in 1907 aged 77. They are buried together in St Nahi's Church graveyard, in Dundrum.

Gerald started his working career in Dublin and was 20 years old when he began to realise his fortune lay elsewhere and considered migrating to New Zealand. There were little prospects of work in Ireland; a legacy left by the Irish potato famine in the mid-1840s and more and more people were choosing migration as a viable alternative. The story goes that he was returning home by train and started talking to a fellow passenger much older than himself who strongly advised him not to go to New Zealand. He mentioned that a number of migrants had chosen Argentina, where land was plentiful, cheap and where immigrants from Ireland were greatly helped by a reception committee who provided information and advice on arrival. Gerald thought seriously about Argentina as an alternative destination and reconsidered his decision to move to New Zealand. With his father's connections in the Church, he was able to obtain a letter of introduction to the Bishop in Argentina. In 1889, at the age of 22 Gerald set sail for Argentina, unconsciously following his ancestral pioneering spirit and call to adventure and continuing the pattern of migration into the next generation.

CHAPTER 2

ARGENTINA

The journey by ship to Argentina across the Atlantic Ocean took between four to six weeks. For migrants with a steerage passage, conditions onboard would have been crowded and the food basic. The voyage would have seemed endless and it must have been with a huge sigh of relief when their ship finally docked in Buenos Aires, the main port of Argentina.

Argentina is the second largest country in South America, spanning 2,795 miles from Tierra del Fuego in the south, to the province of Jujuy and the Tropic of Capricorn in the north. It was named by the Spanish and Portuguese conquerors at the beginning of the 16th century after their first voyages across the South Atlantic Ocean. On reaching the coastline, they sailed up the Rio de la Plata estuary to Buenos Aires, which became the capital city in 1880. The muddy waters flowing into the estuary from the Rio Parana do not do justice to the name River of Silver. It is more likely that the conquerors returned with pockets lined with silver from the indigenous tribes who came down from Bolivia, Peru and Brazil. The name Argentina comes from the Latin word *argentum* meaning silver.

Argentina is a land rich in natural resources and a haven for wildlife, flora and fauna. It has an extreme and varied climate from sub-Antarctic in the south to sub-tropical in the north-east bordering the Brazilian rain forest. Across the central area, vast open plains known as *pampas* stretch for thousands of miles, from the province of Buenos Aires on the east coast, through to the Sierras de Cordoba in the mid-west. The land is completely flat, providing a temperate climate with rich and abundant grazing pastures for horses, sheep and cattle.

Before the arrival of Europeans, *gauchos,* descendants of the original immigrants ruled supreme, staking their claim to thousands of hectares of land capturing wild horses, cattle and sheep and building *estancias,* their farms. They were skilled horsemen and spent their lives in the saddle. They established a law for themselves and carried a long, broad-bladed knife tucked into their wide belts, which they used for settling disputes, chopping wood, killing animals and carving meat to cook on an open fire called an *asado.* They drank a herbal green tea called *yerba mate,* which they brewed in a gourd with hot water, sipping the bitter liquid through a silver straw called a *bombilla.* They tamed wild horses, using saddles made from leather, covered with a blanket and sheepskin, which doubled as bedding when they slept under the stars. They rode holding the reins in one hand, guiding their horses with pressure on the neck, leaving their free hand to lasso animals. They dressed in *bombachas,* baggy trousers made from cotton with wide leather belts around their waists decorated with silver coins and leather ankle boots with elaborate silver spurs. They wore French style berets on their heads and woollen *ponchos* to keep out the cold and rain. *Gauchos* became a legend and continue to have an air of romance and mystery to this day.

Across to the west of the country, the magnificent Andes mountain range forms the western border with Chile, stretching like a spine for 4,500 miles from the southern tip in Argentina through to Bolivia, Peru, Ecuador and Columbia in the north. Mount Aconcagua, in the province of Mendoza, is Argentina's highest mountain at 6,962 metres and the tallest mountain in the southern hemisphere. The lakes and glaciers in southern Patagonia form some of the most magnificent natural landscapes in the world. The sub-tropical forest in the north-east provides wetlands and a haven for birds and other wildlife. Along the north-east border of Argentina, Paraguay and Brazil, the confluence of the Rio Iguazu and the Rio Parana creates the impressive Iguazu Falls, one of the largest natural waterfalls in the world. The eastern coastline bordering the Atlantic Ocean stretches from the estuary of the Rio del la Plata and the port of Buenos Aires, to Ushuaia, the southernmost city in Tierra del Fuego; forming a rich fishing ground and sanctuary for whales, walrus, sea lions, penguins and other marine and wildlife.

It is easy to understand why Argentina was seen as the promised land for the thousands of European migrants who headed to the southern hemisphere to seek their fortunes in this rapidly developing country. At the turn of the nineteenth century Argentina had the potential of being self-sufficient in food, largely due to its natural resources and ample reserves of energy. Immigration was on the increase and by 1904, foreigners contributed to almost 25% of the total population. By 1914, this had risen to more than 30%. Along with the English, Irish and Scottish, the Welsh set up a community in Patagonia, which continues to flourish. From other European countries came the Spanish, French, Portuguese, Dutch, Germans and Italians, who set up their own community in La Boca, a district in Buenos Aires. With little money, they built their houses out of corrugated iron, which they painted in bright colours. It was here the tango was born and is a well-known district in Buenos Aires and the home of a national football team.

At a distance of 6,000 miles from their land of birth, Europeans adopted Argentina as their new homeland. They helped to create a prosperous nation, contributing to the infrastructure of the commercial, banking and finance systems and setting up a railway transport network to cover the vast distances across the country. They designed and built houses, hospitals, department stores, schools and churches in a similar style and architecture of the buildings they had left behind to remind them of home. Generations later, the legacy of the first European immigrants who created the culture and society remains and Buenos Aires is as European a city as London, Paris, Madrid or Rome. It is the only city outside London where Harrods established a satellite store in 1914, which expanded in 1920, but has been closed now for many years.

On his arrival, Gerald joined the hundreds of other immigrants seeking employment. With a letter of introduction in his pocket he was able to find work easily. He had a succession of different jobs, including driving cattle, heading the commissariat attached to the railways and assistant to an *estancia* manager. Around 1898, Gerald was commissioned by a landowner to set up a farming operation on virgin territory not far from the town of Coronel Dorrego, approximately 90 kilometres from Bahia Blanca. He spent the next two years fencing, stocking cattle and installing windmills and water tanks.

On completion of this contract, Gerald sailed for England with a letter of introduction to a businessman in Liverpool who had prospered as a result of dealings in the Chilean nitrate trade and was interested in investing in Argentina. Gerald was commissioned by him to return to Argentina, buy an *estancia* and set it up. On his return Gerald soon found a suitable property of three to four thousand hectares near Bahia Blanca. With finances and a Power of Attorney he duly purchased Estancia El Deseado on behalf of his employer. During the next two years Gerald established El Deseado and felt settled and secure enough to marry. He chose as his bride a young lady of Scottish ancestry living with her family on a neighbouring *estancia*. Maud MacDougall, was born in New Zealand and had migrated to Argentina with her parents around 1886 when she was ten years old. Her father, Robert Douglass MacDougall was born in 1849, the third child of Donald MacDougall who was born in 1811 and Jannett Douglass who was born about 1812. They lived in Braevallich Farm in Argyllshire. Robert was educated at the Dollar Academy in Clackmannanshire and moved to Auchnashellach, Glassary in Argyllshire in 1871. He was a strong-minded and ambitious young man focused on achieving success and decided to migrate to New Zealand for a new and better life.

On arrival in New Zealand, Robert bought land in Ormond, a small town near Gisborne, on the north-east coast of North Island and set himself up as a farmer. He met and married Isabel Best who was born in 1850. Isabel's father, William Best, came from Northumberland and migrated with his family to New Zealand in 1851. He was a farmer and bought land at Grassleas Farm, Tawa Flat, Wellington in North Island. Robert and Isabel married at St Paul's Cathedral, Wellington, on 30 September 1873 and had four children. My grandmother, Maud Douglas; born on 17th June 1876, Evelyn Elizabeth Westwood, born in 1877; Somerled Donald, born in 1879; and Kenneth, born in 1882, who sadly died in infancy.

For some years Robert remained happy with the life he had made for himself and his growing family. Around 1886 for reasons unknown, he decided to leave New Zealand and travel across the Pacific Ocean to Argentina. He clearly saw Argentina as rich farming potential with its flat and abundant pastures and ideal temperate climate. Robert and his family arrived in Argentina with their worldly possessions and a shipload of cattle. He bought an *estancia* with land near Bahia Blanca in the province of Buenos Aires. The family settled into a new life in their new homeland and Maud and Evelyn were educated at a French convent in Bahia Blanca.

Maud was 23 years old when she met Gerald Worthington Brownrigg from El Deseado and they married in Bahia Blanca on 8 May 1900. Among some of my mother's papers, I found a booklet called *The Church Monthly Record for the Church of the Holy Trinity, Lomas de Zamora*. It contained a write up of Gerald and Maud's wedding written by the minister who described his visit to Bahia Blanca to officiate at their marriage, which took place in the Church Room that had been decorated to *"lend grace, beauty and solemnity to the occasion."* He wrote about the reception held at the MacDougall's home and a toast proposed to the *"first British Bride in Bahia Blanca and of the Bridegroom,"* wishing them life-long health and prosperity.

Gerald and Maud settled into married life at El Deseado and within two years the first of their five sons Gerald (Ged) Worthington, was born on 24 July 1902. The following year, Maurice Neville, my father, was born on 8 December 1903. Six years later, Valentine Worthington (Paddy), was born on 12 February 1909, followed by Robert Denis (Bobby), on 13 September 1912 and Herbert Annesley (Bertie), on 25 December 1914. All the boys were born at El Deseado. A copy of my father's birth certificate records his birth at Bolivar, Provincia de Buenos Aires, which was possibly the registration district where El Deseado lay. The location of El Deseado has sadly been lost in time and I have not been able to identify exactly where it was situated.

In 1913 the family travelled to England to arrange education for Ged and Maurice. It was common practice among British immigrants to send their children to school in England because the scanty British schooling in Argentina was considered by many people to be inadequate. Having settled the boys into boarding school, Gerald and Maud returned to Argentina.

The outbreak of the First World War in 1914 separated the family for the next five years, during which time Ged and Maurice spent their holidays with relations or friends. In 1918 when it was safe to travel by sea, Gerald and Maud sailed to England to bring their boys back to Argentina to finish their education at St George's College in Buenos Aires. The boys had left as children and returned as young adults, aged 15 and 16, having lived through a world war.

The Brownrigg Family (1918)
Gerald and Maud with their sons
left to right Paddy (standing), Bobby, Bertie, Ged (seated) Maurice (standing)

In 1920, Gerald began negotiating with his principal to buy El Deseado with the idea of retiring and leaving it in the hands of Ged or Maurice to manage. However, before negotiations were completed, the owner died and his heir sold the property by auction. With their hopes of buying El Deseado dashed, presumably through lack of capital, Gerald and Maud set sail once again for England with their three younger sons. Initially, they stayed with Gerald's sister, Amy Fitzgerald, in Dublin before travelling to England to place the boys into boarding school at Fernden in Haslemere, Surrey. The school was owned and run by Norman Graham Brownrigg, a first cousin of his father's, Robert Graham Brownrigg. With the boys settled, Gerald and Maud returned to Ireland and rented a house in Bray, a seaside resort south of Dublin. The following year they moved back to England and the boys moved to Bedford School where they completed their education. It was always understood the family would go back to Argentina and they returned in 1932, and settled into an apartment in Buenos Aires.

My father, Maurice, began his working life in Buenos Aires in 1921 as an audit clerk with Price, Waterhouse, Faller & Company, where he remained until 1923. He completed his two years of Argentine military service and in 1925 began working as an assistant to *estancia* managers in the western camp in the Western Railway area. He worked for Shell-Mex Argentina Limited in Bahia Blanca from 1930-31 and later joined the railway in a venture involving the collection and transportation of farm produce to railway stations for onward shipment to Buenos Aires. In 1934, he joined the River Plate Trust-Loan Agency in Buenos Aires, the same year his parents and younger brothers returned to Argentina.

In 1940, Maurice's younger brother Paddy invited him to join a weekend shooting party at the Ingenio La Esperanza, where he was working for the Leach's Argentine Estates. Maurice travelled up by train from Buenos Aires and Paddy met him at the station outside the Finca

Los Lapachos, together with Ambrose Alexander, the manager of the Ingenio, and his 20 year daughter, Joan. Maurice was introduced to his hosts and was immediately captivated by the pretty young girl with her dark hair and dark eyes who extended her hand in welcoming him to their home.

CHAPTER 3

MATERNAL

Ambrose Alexander migrated to Argentina in 1904 when he was twenty years old. He was born in Ramsbury, Wiltshire, on 30 October 1884, the son of Henry Nelson Alexander and Elizabeth Phoebe Allen and named after his grandfather, Ambrose Alexander of Ambrose Farm, Ramsbury. Educated at Marlborough College, he trained as an accountant and was looking for work after a period of ill health when by chance he met a friend walking down the street. They engaged in conversation and Ambrose told his friend he was thinking of migrating to New Zealand. His friend had similar ideas and was about to set off for Argentina to join his brother who had been out there for a while and loving it. He suggested to Ambrose he should go with him. Hearing his friend describe Argentina as a land of opportunities and welcoming foreigners and their investments captured Ambrose's imagination. With his training in accountancy, he was confident he could find work easily and decided that Argentina was as good as New Zealand. Within a week he had booked his passage to Buenos Aires and set sail across the oceans for a new adventure in the southern hemisphere.

On arrival in Buenos Aires, Ambrose waited in the queue to have his future assigned to him by the Immigration Officers. With his professional background and training, Ambrose was seen as a fitting employee for the expanding railway industry. By this time, the development of the railways was well underway and a network spanned the country. Until 1948, the six most important railways were British owned. However, once the Argentine State took them over, investment did not continue in the same way. Many of the railway lines eventually closed with a change of focus on improving the nation's roads and intercity highways instead of expanding the railways.

There are no records of which railway company Ambrose worked for, though it is likely he remained in the Province of Buenos Aires. He was made foreman to a team of workers, but not being able to speak Spanish made communication difficult, especially when giving orders and dealing with unruly workers after pay day. Liquor was readily available and drinking in the local *boliche* or bar was a nightly occurrence. Ambrose soon tired of the work and contacted his friend who suggested he join him on the citrus fruit farm and sugar estate at the Ingenio La Esperanza, in Jujuy. Ambrose decided it was a better option and headed north to join his friend arriving at the station in San Salvador de Jujuy, the capital city of the province, where he found a very different landscape to the hot and dusty flat lands of the pampas.

The province of Jujuy lies just under 1000 miles north-west of Buenos Aires in the foothills of the magnificent Andes mountains bordering Chile and Bolivia. It has a sub-tropical climate, sunshine and rain providing the ideal temperature for growing sugar cane and citrus fruits. Spanish colonialism and the indigenous Inca culture live side-by-side, and the architecture of the buildings and the local people called *quechas* or *coyas,* are descendants from the Inca Empire. With their bowler hats and colourful dress, their lives have not changed much during the centuries, despite modern technology and mobile telephones now coming out of the pockets of their multicoloured attire. The *coya* women wear layers of skirts and when it gets cold they simply add another layer. They sit in fields, weaving colourful textiles watching their herds of goats and alpacas, many with babies strapped to their backs with the sound of the panpipes, echoing through the mountain air providing a haunting mystical sense of its ancient past.

Ambrose's friend was working for Leach's Argentine Estates, a company established by five brothers who had arrived from England in the early 1880s. They brought with them engineering expertise and in 1883 helped to build a new sugar mill near San Pedro de Jujuy in the San Francisco Valley. The machinery was shipped from England and transported by ox cart from the railhead in Tucuman, a distance of 400 kilometres. The factory took a year to complete and the first crop was harvested with the help of local indigenous Indians from Bolivia, who were employed to supplement their workforce. A thriving township developed around the Ingenio La Esperanza, attracting more than 100 immigrants from England and other parts of the world. They built houses, schools, a hospital, theatre, a chapel and a zoo and formed sports and social clubs. The Leach family employed many Europeans as well as local people and were well respected among the community for looking after the welfare of their employees. In September 1963, a monument was unveiled to commemorate the Leach brothers on the sixtieth anniversary of the first harvest, in acknowledgement of their contribution to the town.

Ambrose arrived at La Esperanza and joined the company as an accountant and was asked to oversee the Bachelor's Quarters. He liked his new working environment and decided to stay, quickly adapting to his surroundings, learning the language and the management of the estate. It was pioneering work and challenging, especially working with the local indigenous Indian tribes who didn't necessarily get along together, creating rivalry and unrest. For the next seven years, Ambrose worked hard to earn enough money to pay for a passage to England on leave. He must have been feeling lonely and in need of a wife for on his return he married Lillian, a young lady he had met before he left England.

Lillian Winifred Hawkins was born in London on 28 February 1882, the eldest daughter of Amos Hawkins and Emma Eustace. Lillian had two sisters, Nellie and Evelyn Viola (Vio) and two brothers, Bertram and Stanley. Lillian's father, Amos Hawkins, was appointed High Court Tipstaff in the Courts of Chancery in January 1884. My mother told me that her mother, my grandmother, was an actress and a singer, although I never remember her talking about her life on stage or about her family in England. Lillian and her family moved to Cherry Tree Walk in Heronsgate, near Rickmansworth, Hertfordshire around 1890.

My research led me to contact the Rickmansworth Historical Society and I discovered that Heronsgate formed part of Heronsgate Farm, one of the original areas of land adopted by the Chartist Co-operative Land Society by Fergus O'Connor in 1846. In one of the family albums there is a photograph of a house in Cherry Tree Walk, on the back of which my mother had written, *'Mum's home.'* When I made a visit to Rickmansworth, I found Cherry Tree Walk but could not identify the house, although the very narrow lanes and high hedges were similar to those in the photograph.

Ambrose and Lillian were married in London on 28 October 1911, at St Philip's Church, Kensington. Lillian was 29 years old and Ambrose was 27; they had not seen each other for seven years and their only means of communication would have been through writing letters. Lillian arrived at La Esperanza as a young bride and had to adapt to her new life in a strange land thousands of miles from her family and home. With its different landscape, climate, seasons and language, her new homeland provided a stark contrast to the life she had left behind in England. Despite an established community of British and Europeans from similar backgrounds who were living and working at La Esperanza, I have a sense it would have been challenging for her and she must have felt homesick at times for her family and home. Sadly I never thought to ask about her life before she married my grandfather or how she felt as a young bride going to live on the other side of the world. However, I like to think she had a pioneering spirit, a sense of adventure and love in her heart to follow a man she had not seen for seven years to the other side of the world.

Lillian became a housekeeper and helped Ambrose to oversee the Bachelor Quarters. A year later, on 16 October 1912 their first daughter, Viola, was born. A second daughter, Mary, followed on 4 March 1917, who sadly died from infantile gastroenteritis when she was only three months old. Two years later, Lillian became pregnant with her next child. The memory and grief of her lost baby may have made her decide to have her child in England. By now Ambrose had been asked to take over the management of La Esperanza, which necessitated regular trips to England for Board Meetings. It was easy, therefore, to arrange to be in London for the birth of their third child, who was to become my mother.

PART 2

MY MOTHER

"DO YOU SEE, DEARIE? DO YOU SEE THAT?"

"Those are the words I associate with sitting and chatting late into the night with Joan Brownrigg, Kinesiologist extraordinaire. Joan's knowledge was vast and all-embracing to the extent she could appear quite daunting. She brought her huge intellect to bear on all the 'balancing' she did, researching and making notes about the health problems her clients presented, asking them before she saw them what it was they wanted help with. She was always fully prepared and prepared for the unexpected because she kept an open mind about outcomes and she assiduously developed approaches to make sure her muscle testing was as accurate and non-judgmental as possible, using a variety of techniques to do so.

I had some amazing 'balances' with her, as she quietly muscle tested me and asking silent questions or made pertinent comments about whatever issue or problem I had taken to her. At one stage in my life I could only meet her in the evenings and after she had 'balanced' me we talked until the early hours, times I really cherished. When I think of her, I remember her tall, elegant presence, her quiet and authoritative demeanour and her consistent interest in the wellbeing of those people around her. Some of us, sometimes commented on what a beauty she must have been in her youth.

Always respecting confidentiality, she would regale me on those evenings with some of the most incredible stories of what had proved to be the cause of particular problems her clients brought to her. "You'll never believe what happened recently," she would say and proceed to tell me how her muscle testing had led her to some obscure, but highly significant piece of information needed for the healing to be effective. One session she told me about that stuck in my mind was of someone who had been allergic to fruit for as long as she could remember. During the balance Joan had 'age recessed' the client to about the age of two, which turned out to be when her mother had died. There had been a further incident not long before when the client had almost choked on a boiled fruit sweet. The mother had been horrified and impressed on the child not to eat such sweets again. After the balance with Joan however, many years later, the client had been able to eat fruit with no allergic reaction. The significant point about this is not so much the dramatic success of the balance as Joan's meticulous attention to detail, which meant she continued searching for significant messages from the body until she fully identified the underlying cause for a problem.

I remember when I first realised how innovative Joan could be. It was quite early on after we had first learned Touch for Health and after the Open Day at the local library, which our Touch for Health group had organised, where so many people turned up. Joan was one of three Touch for Health Instructors attending that day and there had been much pressure on them to give talks, leaving them exhilarated and exhausted at the end of the day. Joan told me afterwards that she had a breakthrough when she got home and decided to try muscle testing to balance herself after such a momentous day. This is something a number of Kinesiologists practise nowadays, but then it was entirely new. Joan had struck on the original idea of focusing on the Five Element Wheel in the Touch For Health Handbook and tested herself to see where she was off balance and what to do. It worked!

I suspect she must have shared this eureka moment with Charles Benham. They became very good friends through Kinesiology, having much in common personally and in terms of their searching intellects. Charles, of course, went on to develop the very effective, Optimum Health Balance and I'm sure it's partly because he learnt about self-testing from Joan.

My friendship with Joan developed during three phases. First of all we were very active in setting up the Touch for Health Centre in Bognor Regis and I remember some of the wonderful coincidences that led us to feel we were 'going with the flow.' The rooms above a Vet's practice had been recently redecorated and carpeted by the landlord and seven of us had a small amount of money we had pooled. Furniture had been donated - bookshelves, a desk, chair and small tables and we had been given some stacking chairs - but we needed a sink unit. Joan suggested we went to the local scrap merchants as a possibility and unbelievably we found a lovely unit, which exactly fitted our measurements. My husband brought his huge Citroen Estate car and we collected it in time before they closed when my husband was unexpectedly free. No mobile telephones then, so the practicalities were much more complicated.

Joan made the very best of living alone, although I know she missed having her late husband and family close to her. She went on every Kinesiology and healing course she could manage and always took with her a trusty tape recorder. In the evenings she trawled through the cassettes, making notes and checking she had understood everything. I think she worked late into the night. This was probably the second phase of my knowing her. She was such a source of information and generally knew of or possessed a book or several books about many of the issues that interested me. She talked about Arthur, her 'guru' as she called him, who had lived not far from her when the family lived at Earnleys, the home she had loved so much. He had introduced her to the idea of energy work and at about the same time she had, I think, become a regular attender at the 'COMPASS' group; the 'Chichester Open Meeting for Psychic and Spiritual Studies'. Typically, she had become its Librarian and I wouldn't be surprised if she had read most of their books!

Muscle testing - and particularly self-testing - led Joan into areas which some people thought were extreme. Ultimately, she called the type of work she was doing *Guided Kinesiology* because she was convinced she was in contact with a level of intelligence that far surpassed her own. Given her meticulous attention to detail I felt utterly comfortable with some of the more seemingly bizarre things she would tell me. I was privileged to be able to learn from her and very much regretted losing the regular face-to-face contact when I moved away from Sussex to Wales in 2000. We did however, keep in touch by telephone and she demonstrated her ability to tune in at a distance with accurate results. Joan was a source not only of amazing information, but of a consciousness not contained by everyday trivialities or other people's belief systems. She had her peccadilloes but her mind with its originality was a joy to behold.

The third phase of knowing her was the period when I went to her for 'balancing' during a particularly trying time in my life when my marriage was in trouble and I was in the process of going through a divorce. Joan 'balanced' me a number of times, always refusing to take money and spending large amounts of time helping me to sort out deep personal issues. It was extraordinarily generous of her. I trusted her judgment implicitly and on her couch I felt I was in the best possible space. The many resources she kept to hand were all carefully filed and sorted into order and the room felt welcoming and still. I particularly valued her ability to stay centred and not be drawn into my emotional pain. She remained consistently strong and detached while making me feel my concerns were her topmost priority.

She was one day younger than my father, which made our friendship interesting. They were very unalike except for the rather austere bearing they both shared. In my experience, Joan was constant and steady in everything she did and it was a real privilege to have known such a remarkable human being."

Maureen Hardy, retired, Honorary Fellow, Kinesiology Federation.

CHAPTER 4

CHILDHOOD

Lillian and Ambrose's third daughter, Joan Constance, was born on 2 March 1920 in a house in Pennywern Road, Earls Court, London, a few blocks from the church where her parents were married nine years before. It was the home of Lillian's sister, Vio and where the family stayed when they came to England on home leave. It was a typical London terrace house, which still stands to this day, as I discovered when I made a pilgrimage to visit mum's first home. It had a green front door and a gargoyle over the entrance to the basement. It felt strange standing outside her house as I thought of her as a young baby and realising that I too had been born in a city and we were both destined to spend our lives away from the land where we were born.

My mother said she never liked this house and had unhappy memories of her early experiences, some of which she described to me,

"When you entered the house, you came up the stairs, there was a bathroom on the landing, then up some more stairs and my room was opposite the main living room. No one was allowed in here unless they were playing the piano. At night as I lay in bed, with the landing light on all I could see was a great clock by the door, which looked like someone was watching me. I had a horrible nurse who was very strict, she looked like a witch and was always scolding."

Mum described herself as a sickly child and the certificate of her private baptism held in the house dated shortly after she was born indicated that perhaps her parents didn't think she would survive, especially with the memory of their previous infant daughter who died so young. However, despite her fragile beginnings, Joan inherited the family's adventurous, pioneering spirit and strong inner strength that helped her throughout her life. Her parents took her home with them to Argentina, 6000 miles from the land of her birth, when she was three months old. This was the first of many journeys she made crossing the Atlantic Ocean. Argentina became her adopted homeland, which she grew to love with a passion that remained with her all her life.

On their return to La Esperanza with Ambrose's position now as Manager, the family moved to the Manager's house, Las Rosas. It was built in a colonial style of a single-storey house with a central courtyard and veranda running along the outside. The house was approached by an avenue of palm trees and a wide circular drive, surrounded by a large garden with bamboos, roses, shrubs and trees.

Las Rosas

As the Manager's wife, Lillian had plenty of staff to keep the house and garden in order, including a nanny for her daughters. She also had to take on the role of hosting dinner parties and entertaining guests, which she found somewhat taxing. Despite her love of acting, it seems she didn't take to her new role easily, maybe the language barrier made polite conversation difficult.

Growing up in the foothills of the Andes, Joan grew to love the land that became her home. She may have been born in England, but she always felt Argentina was where she belonged. Even so, some of her early childhood memories were deeply painful. She said her mother was frail after her birth and she was looked after by a nanny and she felt the separation from her mother. As she grew older, she was looked after by an unpleasant maid with hypnotic eyes. She said this made her afraid to look anyone in the eye, even into adulthood.

On 25 July 1921, Lillian gave birth to another daughter, Gwen. Sadly, like her little sister, Mary, Gwen died when she was three months old. It is interesting to reflect that my mother always said she was the youngest daughter, which gave the impression Gwen was born before her, rather than after. However, going through some papers after she passed away, I found an envelope containing a small piece of paper on which her mother had written the names and birth dates of Mary and Gwen. Joan was, of course, the youngest surviving daughter.

My mother recounted stories of a number of accidents and falls she had at a young age. On one occasion she was dressed as a fairy for a pantomime and fell off a table, landing on her head. Another time her father was carrying her on his shoulders and she lost her balance and rolled off onto the ground. Her father was a tall man, so it would have been a hard fall. On another occasion, aged about 12 years old, she was sitting in the back seat of a car returning from a visit to a neighbouring *estancia* to see some Arab horses. It was night and the car hit a large trench in the middle of the road, which had not been there when they drove on the same road earlier in the day. In the intervening time, the farmer had dug the trench across the main road to drain the water from one of his fields. He left no warning signs and in the dark the driver did not see the trench and hit it at speed.

The jolt threw my mum from her seat and she hit her head on the crossbar on the roof of the car. She heard her neck crack and said she literally saw stars. The driver was unperturbed at her plight, saying only, *"You are not going to faint, are you, Joan?"* She was told not to fuss because she was conscious and they continued their journey. They were in the middle of the camp with no emergency services on call and she was never taken to see a doctor. What injuries she may have sustained can only be imagined as the crack she heard could have been a fracture in her neck. In later life she suffered with headaches and neck problems, which she maintained were a result of this incident. Another time she fell off a five bar gate, damaging her shoulder and ribs. She was a tomboy at heart and loved climbing trees and taking risks, and accidents were bound to happen and never stopped her from living life to the full.

Joan grew up in an atmosphere of loss and suffering, with the death of her sister, Gwen, which would have affected her as the family grieved the loss of their baby. When she was five years old, her best friend and constant playmate also died, leaving her devastated and heartbroken, made worse by her not being told why she was no longer there to play with her. Also, her little dog and constant companion who slept by her bed suddenly disappeared. She missed her playmate and little dog and when Viola, her elder sister and constant companion to who she was devoted, was sent to school in England, it was as though those she loved were always leaving her. With Viola away at school, her mother became very needy of her younger daughter, saying that she had lost two babies and with another in England, she wanted to keep her close by her side.

Despite the sadness and sorrow, family photographs paint a picture of her early childhood with plenty of smiles and happy times. Her mother taught her to read when she was five years old after she had been given several books that belonged to her friend in her memory. There were plenty of fancy dress parties and other children to play with so she was never left on her own. A favourite pastime was picnics by the river when they all drove off in a car to have fun. Flash floods were common after heavy rain in the summer and a small stream quickly became a raging torrent. On one occasion their car was caught crossing a river and carried downstream, eventually coming to a stop. They had to be pulled out by horses, which left her with a fear of crossing rivers from the memory of drifting downstream out of control.

With her father's love of riding and playing polo, Joan was taught to ride as soon as she was old enough to sit in a chair strapped to the back of a pony. It was the beginning of her love of horses and she became an accomplished rider as she grew up. She loved nothing more than riding with her father around the sugar cane fields and watching him play polo, which was a favourite pastime. The number of cups he won is evidence of his expertise.

Joan (3) sitting in a chair on a horse

Joan loved spending her days outdoors in nature, climbing trees or horse riding. Consequently, her mother despaired of her ever becoming a young lady and learning the skills deemed necessary for someone of her social standing. Despite her mother's worries, Joan had a natural creative talent and learned to knit and sew and crafted many beautiful pictures in embroidered silk. She also loved to draw and paint and spent hours drawing pictures of her beloved horses.

As well as regular trips on home leave to England, holidays in Argentina were taken in the neighbouring province of Salta or Tilcara, a resort in the Humahuaca Valley high in the mountains on the road to Bolivia, where they escaped the heat of the summer. The fortress at Tilcara remains a ruin of the stronghold once used by the indigenous Indians, against the Spanish conquerors. From its position on top of a hill, it holds a commanding view over the valley, surrounded by giant cacti and the landscape has not changed since those times.

On their trips to England on home leave, they also visited Lillian's mother, who had moved to France. My mother had a strong memory of these visits because she remembered her grandmother having ulcerated legs, which were covered in bandages and left a lasting impression on her. She also remembered falling and grazing her knee and being held down while the knee was treated because the bandage stuck to the wound. Her young cousins were visiting at the same time, but did not want to play with her or include her in their games because she was too little which left her feeling lonely and rejected.

CHAPTER 5

SEPARATION AND LOVE

Apart from visiting family on home leave, England also meant school and education. The local education in Argentina was not considered good enough and sending children to school in England around the age of eight years old was the chosen option for many families. While their education may have benefitted, many children were left deeply traumatised by the separation from their parents, homes and families at such a young age.

Ambrose and Lillian sent Viola to an English boarding school and then onto finishing school in Switzerland. Fortunately for Joan, this fate did not come for her until she was 14 years old. Before that she had a series of governesses, although she found them demanding and her education was spasmodic. It was Lillian's reluctance to part with her daughter that kept her by her side for as long as possible. Eventually, Ambrose persuaded her that Joan needed to complete her education in England and with heaviness of heart she had to agree to let her go. They chose Roedean School in Brighton, Sussex, being close to where Ambrose's sisters, Alex and Sealy, lived in Hove, thinking she would be able to weekly board and be looked after by family. However, at the last minute they changed their minds in favour of Hamilton House, a boarding school in Tunbridge Wells, Kent, where the daughter of a friend of theirs was a pupil. They thought she would be a friendly face for Joan to help her settle. However, the girl was older and their paths rarely crossed.

Joan (14) with her parents, Ambrose and Lillian

Joan did not take to her new life at an English boarding school easily and disliked the school intensely. This was her first experience of being away from home and her family and she was very homesick and unhappy. She missed her family and friends, but most of all she missed her homeland and the life she was used to and the freedom that offered. Being from another country with a different background and culture and speaking with a different accent from her classmates and teachers, made her feel isolated and alone. She felt she had nothing in common with the other girls and her intermittent education made her feel inadequate, stupid and a complete ignoramus compared to her peers.

During her second term, her inner tears of sadness developed into double pneumonia. Talking about it later, she admitted that she had hated it so much she had made herself ill and she nearly died. Her illness affected the whole school as the girls had to wear gym shoes and the clocks were not allowed to chime to maintain a quiet environment. Without modern antibiotics, her body had to heal itself. Unfortunately, her parents could not travel to be with her because Ambrose also became ill at the same time and needed to go to Buenos Aires for treatment. Her father's sister,

Aunt Sealy became her surrogate mother and stayed with her night and day, gradually nursing her back to health through her love, care and complete devotion. A strong bond was formed between them and they always remained very close. After six weeks, Joan was well enough to be allowed home to convalesce and went to stay with Aunt Sealy. She was very weak and needed a bath chair to be taken on walks along the sea front, the sea air and sunshine helping to restore her health. As soon as Ambrose was well enough to travel, he and Lillian set sail for England. Her first question to her father as soon as they met was, *"Can I go back to Argentina now?"* He firmly said, *"No, you must complete your education. You can return when you pass your School Certificate and not go onto finishing school like your sister."*

Joan had a lifeline, but she had to return to the school she hated. Luckily, it was near the end of the summer term and she had holidays to look forward to. As she was not allowed to play games, she was given the chance to take up riding instead. Being back in the saddle made school not so bad after all and she quickly settled into focusing on her studies to pass her exams. Three years later, her commitment and hard work paid off. She passed all her exams and was awarded her University of Oxford School Certificate passing with credit in six subjects, as well as the Royal Drawing Society Full School Certificate with Honours in all six divisions. She had earned her reward and at last she could go home!

This determination to succeed was to follow her all her life. Whatever she did, she did it with focus and precision, moving beyond what was expected of her. She pushed her own boundaries and thus achieved far more than her initial expectations. She remained humble in her progress and never sought acknowledgement nor the recognition she richly deserved, despite all her achievements.

As soon as her exams were over and the school term ended, Joan was on a ship back to Buenos Aires. She had left as a child and returned as a tall, elegant young lady aged 17. She was so happy to be home and the freedom and joy she felt being back in La Esperanza was a sharp contrast to the restrictions and sadness she had felt while at school in England. She now had her own personal maid who ran her bath, fixed her clothes and looked after her every need. Her horse was saddled ready for her daily ride and she reconnected to the land she loved in the way that she loved.

Joan (19) on horseback

From the stories she told, she spent most days riding, going to parties, having picnics by the river and meeting plenty of young men ready and willing to sweep her off her feet. Her first love was Pancho, who was much older than her. They first met when she was only 14 years old. She never said so, but perhaps her parents sensed a schoolgirl crush, which hastened their decision to send her away to school. No doubt she wrote to him regularly while they were apart and perhaps dreamed they might get married one day. However, she said on her return home when she saw him again, she knew he was not the one she wanted to marry.

Joan was more interested in finding a career rather than settling down to marriage and family life. Since childhood, she had wanted to study medicine and be a doctor and she spent hours reading medical books and learning about the workings of the human body. Her passion came from an experience she had when she was seven years old. On one of her visits to England with her parents she was taken to a Spiritualist church with her aunts. The service included powerful healing and she witnessed this taking place through the laying-on of hands which moved to tears and she cried for days afterwards. Her aunts were concerned saying, *"She has been moved by the spirits"* and they thought it unwise to take her again. But something happened to her that day, and from then on she thought of nothing else except finding a way to work in a healing profession when she was older. However, her parents did not want their daughter to enter a profession and discouraged her from having a career. It was not customary in those days for women to work as they were expected to get married and have a family. Her sister Viola had married Frank Wesley Leach, the son of Frank Leach, one of the founder members of the Leach Argentine Estates, on 1 September 1932, and their daughter, Diana, was born in London in February 1934. Joan was expected to find a husband, settle down and raise a family in a similar way. Joan soon realised there was no way of getting around her parents on the subject of a career. However, she found another way to follow her heart and began volunteering at the local hospital, always hoping one day she would find a way to follow her passion.

Joan was 20 years old when she met the man she was destined to marry. She had accompanied her father and Paddy Brownrigg, who worked at La Esperanza, to greet his brother, Maurice, who had been invited to join them for a weekend shooting party. Maurice was a very accurate rifle shot, as was Joan. Ambrose, Paddy and Joan stood on the platform waiting for the train to arrive from Buenos Aires. The train pulled into the small station alongside the Finca Los Lapachos, and a handsome man with fair hair and blue eyes stepped off the train and walked down the platform towards them. Paddy welcomed his brother and introduced him to Ambrose and Joan. As Joan and Maurice shook hands, their eyes met and something drew them together, it was almost love at first sight. Despite their age difference, Maurice was 37, they fell in love and became engaged in April 1940.

Joan and Maurice were married on 16 April 1941 at St John's Pro-Cathedral in Buenos Aires and their wedding was reported in the society pages of the Buenos Aires Standard,

'Fashionable and pretty, the bride made a charming picture in her simple gown of white and silver cloquet, cut on classical lines. The bodice was buttoned down the back and slightly draped in front, the spreading skirt continued to form a circular train and both her delicately embroidered veil of tulle d'illusion and the halo headdress of orange blossoms were loaned to her by the bride's sister.'

The ceremony was followed by a reception for the large number of guests at the English Club and their honeymoon was spent at the fashionable seaside resort of Punta del Este, in Uruguay.

Following their marriage, the happy couple lived in an apartment in Buenos Aires, near to Maurice's office at the River Plate Trust & Company on Avenida de Mayo. Joan volunteered at the British Hospital in Buenos Aires in the Ear, Nose and Throat department. She also found time to enter the world of fashion as a model for charity at the Casa Tow Fashion Parade in the Plaza Hotel and the high-class department store, Harrods, in Calle Florida. Joan had the figure of a model with beautiful features and she was often taken to be a film star. She also helped fund-raise for charity and in December 1941, Liberty Fair was held in the Hurlingham Club to raise money for the British Red Cross and St Dunstan's Hostel for the War Blinded. Pictures in the Buenos Aires Standard showed her busy at work at the top of a ladder helping set up one of the stands. Clearly Joan was able to lend a hand and undertake any task asked of her, whether modelling fashion, painting or woodwork. She had a natural talent and was always willing to try something new.

CHAPTER 6

VOLUNTARY SERVICE - TOGETHER

Life in Argentina continued to unfold for the newly married couple, while back in England war in Europe dominated the lives of their families and loved ones. Despite the great distance between the two countries and Argentina's neutrality, the duty and responsibility felt for their homeland remained strong. After war was proclaimed, patriotism and love for the motherland saw more than 700 men and women of the Anglo-Argentine community sign up as volunteers for the British Armed Forces. Among these were Maurice and his brothers, as well as many of their friends. Not wanting to be parted from her new husband, Joan also signed up as a volunteer.

A new chapter unfolded in their lives as they handed their lives over to His Majesty's Armed Forces. They were no longer certain of their future together or could make plans like other newly married couples. Maurice originally volunteered to join the Navy because he knew someone in the British Embassy who could arrange the paperwork. They booked their passage to England, but the paperwork wasn't ready in time and the ship sailed without them. When news reached them that this ship had been torpedoed with a total loss of life, they must have felt fate had played a hand by delaying their passage due to the bureaucratic process of paperwork. To avoid further delays, Maurice decided to apply for the Royal Air Force instead. Another passage was booked in anticipation the papers would come through in time. This time there were no delays and the documents arrived before the ship was due to sail.

On 24 October 1942, Maurice and Joan set sail on the SS Highland Princess, bound for war-torn Europe. They were travelling with Maurice's brother, Bobby and many of their friends. They stood on deck waving goodbye to their families and friends as the ship pulled away from the quayside, with a sense of the unknown uppermost in their minds. They must have wondered what they were letting themselves in for and feeling mixed emotions of sadness, fear and courage, as well as excitement and anticipation at their new adventure, along with doubts and questions about what had made them leave the comfort and safety of a peaceful existence to enter a war zone. Without knowing what life had in store for them, they could only hope and pray for a safe return. As they ventured into the unknown, it must have been hard for them knowing that life in Argentina for their family and friends would continue as normal.

Joan and Maurice had experienced separations from their families during their school years, but they never found it easy to be parted from loved ones. During World War I, Maurice and his brother had spent four years apart from their family when they were at school in England and were unable to return to Argentina until the war ended. They had already experienced what it was like to live through a war, yet now they would be in the front line rather than being kept safe and protected, as they had been as young boys. Joan and Maurice came from close-knit loving families and the separation was hard for them all. With each new departure and with every passing year, the sadness continued to build. It was not something they could change and could only accept it was part of the life they had chosen and keep their deepest feelings hidden rather than openly shed tears.

Within hours of their ship leaving the quayside, Joan distracted herself by writing her first letter home to post it from Montevideo, their first port of call.

The last time she had been there, she and Maurice were on their honeymoon, happy and excited as a newly married couple. Now they were going to war and sadness replaced the joy in their hearts. The contrast couldn't have been more extreme. Writing about their new experiences helped her connect to her loved ones and her letters were passed round the family to keep them up-to-date with their news. Her letters provided a glimpse into a period of their lives that was dark and dangerous, not only for them but also for all those people who were fighting for their country. They had chosen to leave the safety of their homeland to face challenges and difficulties they could not talk about because letters were censored. Despite writing as positively as she could, so much was left unsaid and there was an underlying grief and desperation as she began the journal of her new life. Letters were to become her salvation because it was the only way she could stay close to her loved ones during what came to be the darkest period in her young life.

She did her best to write with lightness of spirit to hide the depth of sadness she was feeling, although it clearly broke her heart to leave them with the uncertainty of what lay ahead. She focused on describing her first impressions of life on board and how they entered the Forces as soon as they set foot on the ship and were assigned tasks and duties to get them accustomed to a life of duty in service. Men and women were segregated into different sleeping quarters, with bunks crammed into each cabin with hardly room to move. They had to sleep with the cabin doors open in case the boat was torpedoed, as well as wear life jackets all the time and carry their support kit wherever they went. They were up at dawn for daily exercises and lifeboat drill, which meant a jump from the deck of the ship into the lifeboat as it swung precariously over the side of the ship above the rolling surf. To lose one's nerve and footing would have certainly resulted in falling into the sea with potential loss of life. There were so many new experiences and with the ship weaving across the oceans dodging U-boats, they must have wondered more than once what had made them want to leave the warmth and comfort of the home they had left behind. They travelled with many friends which helped keep their spirits up and together they had a lively social time on board. Even so, it must have been with a sense of relief when they reached their final destination having made it safely across the oceans.

Their ship docked in Ireland and Joan and Maurice retrieved their belongings, except for Joan's bicycle, which could not be found. They travelled onto London to stay with Aunt Vio and from there journeyed down to Hove to stay with Aunt Alex and Aunt Sealy. They were welcomed into the loving arms of their English family, which must have made them feel comforted and supported after their long journey.

A few days later, they returned to London and began the official process of enrolling in His Majesty's Armed Forces. Joan also intended to sign up for the Royal Navy, but found the Buenos Aires Consular recommendation was for the Women's Auxiliary Air Force (WAAF) and she joined the Royal Air Force with Maurice. Apart from Ged who remained in Argentina managing the *estancia*, Maurice's brothers also volunteered. Paddy and Bertie signed up for the Royal Air Force and became Pilot Officers; Bobby signed up for the Army and Royal Artillery and was sent to Wales for his initial training. Maurice was accepted for training as an Airfield Controller and later received his commission as a Pilot Officer. Joan chose to train as a Wireless Operator and was sent to Gloucester to get kitted out in uniform before reporting for preliminary training at a base near Lancaster on the north-west coast of England.

After completing the process of paperwork, they stayed with the family in London before returning to the aunts in Hove to await their orders. The loving support of their family helped to settle their nerves as they reflected on the decisions they had made and the daunting prospect of the path they had chosen. Both families were exceptionally kind and loving towards them and willingly opened up their homes for the young couple throughout the war years. Joan especially spent as much time as she could with them, whenever she had leave. For her, their home became a place of refuge, where she escaped from service life and enjoyed some home comforts.

It didn't take long before their orders came in. Joan reluctantly left the loving arms of her husband and comfort of a home and experienced her first taste of life in the WAAF at the training camp near Gloucester. She wrote about her journey and first night in the camp sleeping on a straw mattress in a cold, draughty dormitory. A sharp contrast to what she had known. After medicals and inspections of every sort and going through the interview and documentation for the course she wanted to take, she was distressed to find out that wireless operators could not get a commission. She said had she known this was not possible, she would have chosen another discipline. However, it was too late to change and she had to accept her only option was to make the best of it. She did have concerns the course involved a large amount of technical knowledge, which she hoped she could cope with, however, this only made her wonder even more what on earth she was letting herself in for. She found the separation from Maurice very hard and missed him terribly.

After being kitted out in Gloucester, Joan left for her preliminary training to a camp in Lancashire. The journey by bus and train was long and tiring. She eventually arrived at her destination and was billeted out to a boarding house with other new recruits. She felt terribly homesick and going through the medicals and initial training in the cold and wet didn't boost her confidence or lift her spirits. Neither did she have any news of Maurice, which only added to her sense of loneliness and despair. By now it was early December and the thought of Christmas so far away from her family and loved ones, made her feel desperately lonely and she longed to be back with them all, enjoying Christmas in the summer sunshine. She said Christmas Day was the most miserable she had ever experienced and survived with the help of letters received from Maurice and her family. Despite her loneliness, she accepted that new experiences take time to get used to and as she began forming friendships, she gradually became used to her new life.

As Joan settled into service life, Maurice began his training at a camp in the West Country. He wrote daily to his wife, a practice he continued throughout the years they were apart. He knew from the beginning that he was destined for overseas service and until his orders came in, they arranged leave together as much as they could, spending time with family in London and Hove. As the training progressed, Maurice discovered he was colour blind, which dashed his hopes of flying and he was uncertain which trade he could enter.

Joan's initial training lasted several weeks during which time she continuously questioned the wisdom of her decision, especially when rising before dawn in the cold and ice of mid-winter. On the whole, she was managing to stand up to the new ordeals but she realised that her new experiences were changing her so much she would never be the same again. Despite her initial doubts about what she was doing and her abilities for carrying them out, she clearly made a mark and was chosen Acting Corporal, at the end of her training period. This entitled her to march alongside squads shouting orders, which she said felt strange, but a treat to be able to do the shouting instead of being shouted at, which she said had *"made her blood boil"* until she got used to it.

Early in January 1943, her preliminary training ended and she was assigned to a base in Wiltshire to begin training as a wireless operator. Another long and arduous train journey took her down to the southern counties. More medicals, inspections and physical training in the freezing cold only added to her discomfort, which made her question the wisdom of signing up in winter. But as she said, *"With a war on, you have to forget about oneself and personal preferences,"* although had she known what she was letting herself in for, she doubted very much she could have made the supreme effort of signing up at all. On the other hand, she realised that not knowing was the best option apart from wondering if civilian work might have been easier and less arduous.

Joan hoped her leave periods would coincide with Maurice's leave during the six months of her training. She could not bear the thought of not seeing him and was already finding their constant separation *"hateful"* which only became worse as the months passed. They met up as and when they could but arrangements could only be made through letters or telegrams, which did not allow for last minute changes of plans. On one occasion, Maurice received a new posting and was uncertain he could get leave so Joan did not put in her own request for leave. Nonetheless, Maurice applied for leave, which was granted much to his surprise. He immediately sent Joan a telegram but she had to wait until the following day to put in her application, which was granted. She immediately sent a telegram to Maurice and left for London. She waited for him to appear at the agreed time and place, but he did not turn up. In desperation, she went to the family home but no one was there. Instead she found a note saying they had gone to a friend's house, where she arrived in a complete state of stress and worry to be told that Maurice had gone to meet her at her camp so they could travel to London together because their time together would be so short. He had wired Joan to tell her, but she had not received the telegram before she left the camp and so she didn't know he was on his way to meet her. Their paths had crossed on the train and she felt sick that so much time had been wasted.

Another time they had arranged to meet and Maurice did not arrive. Joan heard that the railway line had been bombed and feared the worst. Maurice arrived a day late because his train had been cancelled, but there was no way of making contact in the meantime. Eventually, they got together, but it emphasised the continual emotional strain they were under. The constant anxiety about getting together added to the stressful lives they were leading and they longed to be back in Buenos Aires setting up home and enjoying their life as it used to be.

Joan's loneliness without her husband and family constantly filled her with despair of being able to cope. News from home only added to her worries because her mother and Maurice's father had been ill, which made the distance between them seem even greater. Despite the news of their illness, however, the family were enjoying the summer sunshine on the beach in Punta del Este, which made her feel more homesick than ever as she sat wrapped in blankets shivering in her freezing hut in mid-winter.

As Joan contemplated her new life, she began to realise how fortunate she had been with all the luxuries she had taken for granted and how she would certainly appreciate everything all the more when she returned to her normal life again. She especially missed the little things and daily activities, such as: having a meal at a table covered with a table cloth; sitting in an armchair instead of a hard backless bench; stepping out of bed onto a mat; keeping warm with a hot water bottle at night; sleeping in a bed big enough to turn over in; eating a meal with a clean plate for each course; relaxing in a hot bath; and going out at night and actually seeing where she was going. A list, which she said could have gone on and on. Even though it sounded as though she was going through some sort of nightmare, she did her best to comfort her family by saying that on the whole she felt quite content, but she longed for the day when it would all end.

Training was arduous. Every spare minute was taken up with studying or marching, which left little time for letter writing. Within two weeks, she had moved up a class. She found the technical side of the course challenging, yet gradually as her confidence increased, so did her marks. She began to make friends and had met other girls from Argentina. They were given distinctive flashes to wear on their sleeves indicating they were volunteers, which caused a number of comments because they were few and far between.

As Joan became more used to her environment, she began venturing out more, walking into the nearby town with friends and finding the time passing quickly. An overnight pass was coming up and this raised her spirits. She took the train to London to visit Aunt Vio. Unfortunately, Maurice was unable to get leave at the same time, although he hoped to be able to join her the following weekend when she had another 48 hour leave. They stayed together overnight in London with the family before taking the train down to Hove. It was wonderful to be with each other again and the two days flew by. They found each other looking well and despite the service life, both had put on weight. As Joan said, her appetite was tremendous and they seemed to spend the whole weekend leave eating. They picked up letters from home to learn that Maurice's father was recovering from an operation and her mother was having problems with her hearing and she and her father were staying in the Cordoba hills for a spell of mountain air.

Joan felt sympathy for her mother because she was also having problems with loss of hearing from a cold that had affected her ears. She had visited the camp doctor and went to see the family doctor when she was in Hove, who told her it was catarrh and was nothing to worry about. However, when Joan returned to camp, her cold worsened and she ended up confined to bed with a sore throat and a very painful ear. She was not in the best of spirits and with another weekend leave coming up, she was afraid she would not be able to make it unless by some miracle she improved quickly. She was also concerned about missing lessons because she knew it might mean she would have to be re-classed. Also, her birthday was nearing and she had planned a party with her friends, except the way she was feeling she was doubtful if it would take place. She was feeling truly miserable. Unfortunately, the ear infection worsened and the doctors feared she would need a mastoid operation to relieve the pressure in her ear. She was admitted to hospital, and thankfully the abscess broke of its own accord. But she had to spend her birthday in a hospital bed, feeling wretched with no one around to lift her spirits. Her weekend leave had to be cancelled, which added to her misery. She received encouraging news from home that her mother was improving but the more she thought about her family and being stuck in a hospital bed alone on her birthday, the sadder and more despairing she became. And then, much to her surprise, Maurice and Bobby turned up to wish her a Happy Birthday which immediately brought back her smiles and cheered her up considerably.

Joan remained in hospital for several weeks as her ear took its time to heal. This gave her a chance to rest and catch up with her letter writing. She anticipated she would be given a few days sick leave before she had to return to her training. Apart from the wonderful unexpected visit from Maurice and Bobby, her greatest comfort was receiving letters from her family and she eagerly awaited the arrival of the post every morning. The other highlight of her hospital stay was the mobile library once a week and she spent her time reading and writing letters. However, she was becoming increasingly worried she was missing so much training and consequently would have to re-do the course, which would mean staying behind from her group. The thought of having to go back to the beginning did not fill her with joy. Perhaps of more concern was that her left ear was still very deaf and she was afraid she might not be allowed to continue as a wireless operator, which required perfect hearing. Meanwhile, Maurice wrote to say he had been recommended for a commission and would be coming out of the ranks, which made her feel better. Eventually, she was well enough to be discharged from hospital, even though she had loss of hearing in her left ear. She was given a week's leave to convalesce and hoped her hearing would recover in time to enable her to continue her training. She made her way to Hove, where Maurice was able to join her. It was wonderful for her to be out of hospital and back with family again and she made the most of being pampered and being looked after, which helped her recover her health and wellbeing.

Joan returned to camp and quickly settled back into the routine. However, she had missed so much training, she had to be re-classed and repeat some of the coursework, which meant she was no longer with her original group of fellow trainees. Her hearing had still not fully recovered and she missed much of what went on in class. Even so, she was gratified to find she had not totally forgotten all she had learned. On her first day back, they had a surprise test and she managed to get a reasonable mark, despite the fact she had not opened a book for more than a month. She knew with exams due soon, she had a lot of catching up to do.

Following a medical assessment, however, she was devastated to be told her hearing was not good enough to continue training as a wireless operator. She was terribly upset because she had hoped her ear was healing sufficiently for full hearing to be restored, despite the perpetual noise of what she called *"steam engines"* in her ear. She went to see another doctor who changed her treatment which improved her hearing considerably. She was told if the improvement continued, she would be able to continue her training. Some good news at last!

Joan found her marks for the procedure tests were increasing and she was top of the class. Her hearing continued to cause problems and she made weekly visits to the Medical Officer. She continued to focus on her studies and work towards her final exams. Her confidence rose as she maintained good marks and was able to keep her position at the top of her class. As a result, she began to consider her options at the end of the course and wondered whether to apply for a form of high-speed signalling, even though this would mean further training in London. Her finals were looming when Maurice wrote to tell her he had passed his exams and was on track to finish his training and get a commission as a Pilot Officer. His good news gave her hope that she could also do well.

The day of the Final Board arrived and Joan nervously entered the examination room with her peers. As well as a written examination, everyone had to take individually practical speed tests on sending and receiving Morse Code. The written examination was conducted in a large classroom and speed tests on a separate table at the front of the room. As Joan sat writing with deep focus and intent, unbeknown to her Maurice had received his commission and was on his way to give her the news and also to tell her he was being posted overseas. He arrived at the camp and spoke to the Commanding Officer. In the examination room everyone had completed the written examination and Joan was called up first to take the speed tests. She passed Level 1 and was told to complete Level 2 at a faster speed straightaway, which surprised her because she was expecting to do this in the afternoon. The other girls were told to sit and wait for her to finish. She could not understand why she was being asked to do this on her own and she said the additional stress made it harder to focus. She completed both Levels and told to report to the Commanding Officer. She entered his office and was surprised and delighted to find Maurice standing there waiting to see her. The Commanding Officer told her she had to complete both speed tests before she could leave the room and he could think of no other way of getting her to finish her exams and see Maurice in the shortest possible time. However, her initial joy at seeing Maurice and completing her finals was dashed when he gave her the news he was being posted overseas.

Joan was granted leave of absence to spend their last few days together not wanting to think about what this separation would mean. The last seven months had been hard enough, but at least they had been able to see each other now and again and daily letters helped to make things easier. She had always hoped that once Maurice received his commission, they might be posted to the same camp and be together, but his imminent departure shattered all hopes of that ever happening. They were now facing an uncertain future with no knowledge of when they would be able to be together.

Joan and Maurice in RAF uniform

CHAPTER 7

VOLUNTARY
SERVICE - APART

In August 1943, Maurice set sail into the unknown leaving Joan feeling desolate and alone. All she could do was bury her feelings and focus on her own life to deaden the pain in her heart. For months there was no news, which did nothing to ease the sense of loss and sadness at their separation. Unable to disclose his destination, Maurice devised a code in his letter whereby he could indicate where he was. Eventually, the longed-for letter arrived and from the way he began, Joan knew he was in India. Maurice was posted to 84 Squadron and served the next three years in India and Burma in the Intelligence Arm of the Squadron, achieving promotion as a Flying Officer in March 1944.

Despite the stress and intense experience of her finals, Joan's hard work resulted in her passing her exams with flying colours and she received a promotion from Aircraft Woman to Leading Aircraft Woman. She described this as an unusual event in the annals of the Signals School for it had only produced six other LACWs in the four years of its existence. Her name was added to the Roll of Honour as the seventh trainee to pass from the school with such distinction. The news spread throughout the camp causing great excitement as Joan became the centre of attention, much to her embarrassment especially when the Officer in Charge called out her name before the whole school and commended her on her achievement, which ended with three cheers! She excitedly wrote to her family telling them the news and her letter was published in the Buenos Aires Herald.

After her excellent results, Joan was offered the opportunity of becoming an instructress at the school. However, the idea of having to teach all day, especially the technical side, did not fill her with enthusiasm especially as it would have meant another three months' training. She turned the offer down and was posted to an aerodrome near London, which gave her some relief because it meant she could be nearer her family. With her husband away, she needed them more than ever. Joan found it difficult to adjust to life without him, feeling totally lost and hard not to focus on their separation. They had met up only eight times during the seven and half months they were in England together, of which only three of these were for more than 36 hours. Writing to each other every day had kept their time apart bearable but with the war in the Far East taking Maurice even further away, life must have seemed very dark and even more uncertain.

Joan found being closer to London cushioned the pain of being apart from Maurice. She adopted her coping skills mechanism by writing home to her family as positively as she could, always doing her best to cover her feelings of despondency to allay their worries about her, even though it was hard for her to keep cheerful. She found her new posting a welcome change with the shorter shift hours, more leave and better accommodation, which helped her settle into her new environment with relative ease. Her mislaid bicycle had finally caught up with her, which she used to travel the short distance to base camp and this made getting around easier. Independent means of transport was a great help and she referred to her bicycle as her *"iron steed."* More frequent periods of leave meant she visited her family more often and she soon felt completely at home with them.

Joan settled into her new role and was recommended for a commission. She chose a Signals Commission one of the most difficult to achieve because the standard of education was high. This meant she had to sign up for extra Maths lessons to reach the required standard. Unfortunately, she was turned down due to insufficient experience, which left her feeling bitterly disappointed. Again, she wondered if she would have fared better by doing civilian work because life seemed less stressful out of uniform, at the same time she realised all she could do was accept the inevitable and get on with her chosen path. To help raise her spirits, she decided to apply to live off base, which was granted. She found accommodation with cousins from her father's family who lived nearby in Hendon within easy distance for her to commute by bicycle. They were happy to have her stay with them, although their house was small and she had to sleep on a garden lounge chair in the children's playroom. Even so, she was happier living with them and welcomed the change from living on camp, except when she had to sleep on chairs in a cold and draughty control room whenever she was on duty in the early morning and then she questioned the wisdom of her decision.

She worked shift hours and whenever she had more than 24 hours leave, she travelled into London to stay with Aunt Vio, who was now living in an apartment in Putney overlooking the River Thames. Other times she made the journey down to Hove to stay with her aunts who continued affording her the love she missed so desperately from her family in Argentina and her husband in India. Nonetheless, her lifeblood remained the letters and food parcels she received from her loved ones who sent her chocolate and sweets and other luxury goods out of reach for her during the war, which she generously shared with her English family.

Patriotism ran high among the British in Argentina who were united in supporting the war effort in England, especially as it became clear that the greatest need was for more aeroplanes. In October 1940, the Fellowship of the Bellows was formed by the younger members of the

British Community. They were the sons and daughters of first, second, and third generations born in the country to raise money for the Royal Air Force. With the idea that a bellow increases wind and this would add profit to the fund, they adopted an anonymous and humorous approach with names such as, The Keeper of the Wind Bag (Accountant), The Receiver of the Windfalls (Cashier), The Whirlwinds and the Windlass (Secretariat). The idea was for members to pay one cent for every enemy plane brought down during a month, according to figures confirmed by the Air Ministry. Members became Whiffs and could rise in rank to Puffs, Gusts and Hurricanes depending on their contribution. The idea quickly gained momentum and during the first year more than 60,000 members joined the Fellowship and a further 35,000 in the second year. By the end of the war, it had been adopted throughout other countries in South America, as well as in Australia, New Zealand and South Africa. A considerable amount of money was raised through membership fees and other fund raising events and all the money went towards paying for new aircraft. By the end of the war, the total amount collected by the United Fellowship amounted to more than nine million Argentine pesos, of which Argentina had contributed more than one third of the total amount raised.

Joan continued to write home regularly keeping the family up-to-date with her news, although never mentioning her work, which was strictly confidential. In Maurice's absence, her brothers-in-law, Bobby and Bertie, dutifully saw her as often as they could coincide their leave together. Her letters depicted life more like that of a social butterfly rather than as a member of the armed forces, as she recounted her stories of meeting up with friends and family in London and Hove, seeing the latest movies or West End shows, eating out in cafes and restaurants, going to night clubs, catching trains, hitch-hiking and riding her bicycle through all weather. Her letters sounded as though she was on holiday rather than living through a war. She tried so hard to make her life sound as happy and positive as she could to cover up the depths of the sadness and sorrow she was feeling and the longing for the days when her only worry was whether or not the roast meal would be edible. That she desperately missed her loved ones were the unspoken words between the lines in all her letters. As hard as she tried to keep positive, now and again she let slip how she couldn't wait until the war would end and they could return home and be together again. Without her family and aunts providing her with a home-from-home, her life would have been very different. Their love for her kept her going and they looked forward to her visits as much as she did. Their home was the only place where she could relax and find some peace amid the darkness and chaos of war.

As Joan reflected on her first year in service, she could not believe how much had happened nor remember an unhappier one. She enjoyed the company of her brothers-in-law and was delighted when Bertie married a young English girl, Rosanne, leaving Bobby as her sole escort. They had fun together and loved going to the movies or a show, eating in their favourite restaurants and often ended up in a night club before catching the first train or bus home at daybreak. Bertie and Bobby were eventually posted overseas and their brother, Paddy, also served in India in Intelligence and met up with Maurice. Although, they never realised until after the war they were doing the same job in the same area, within a few miles of each other. Paddy had also met an English girl, Suzanne, who was serving in the WAAF and they were now married.

Joan felt lost and alone without her escorts and began socialising more with her colleagues when off duty. She was enjoying her work more and the company of her team. On a day's leave with a friend, they watched the Battle of Britain parade and were very excited when King George VI and Queen Elizabeth came out to take the salute barely 100 yards from where they were standing.

Back home in Argentina, Ambrose had retired from his position as Chairman and Managing Director of Leach's and he and Lillian had left La Esperanza and were temporarily living at the Hurlingham Club. Their intention had been to return to England, but the war meant they had to put their plans on hold. Ambrose was not content to sit around with his years of experience and in December 1943, he decided to brave the oceans and travel to England and look for a job. On his arrival, he went to Hove to stay with his sisters, Alex and Sealy and then travelled to London to be reunited with his daughter who was overjoyed with the unexpected news of his arrival in England. They had a wonderful reunion and met up as often as Joan could get leave.

The war in Europe was reaching a climax and with nightly air raids, Joan took to sleeping under the table. Night after night the bombs were dropped, Joan merely referring to them as *'annoying things'* in her letters so as not to overly concern her family who must have been extremely worried as they read the reports in the newspapers or listened to the news on the wireless. The reality of the noise of the Doodle Bugs suddenly cutting out and knowing the bomb would land in seconds nearby, was something she was not willing to share. Even so in one of her letters she described a bomb that landed in a field next to her base camp and the blast carried away tiles and windows. Another time one landed on the base itself, sending everyone into shelters to escape the debris from the explosion. She had another near miss when she had been told to report to another aerodrome, but the order was immediately cancelled as soon as she arrived and she was told to return to her base camp. She later heard the aerodrome had been bombed and everyone in the tower killed. On another evening as she was cycling along the edge of the aerodrome on the way to report for her shift, a bomber with its engines on fire flew overhead trying to land and crashed right in front of her. She was one of the first to reach the wreckage and witnessed the trauma of death and destruction as ammunition exploded and bullets buzzed around her sounding like bees. The rescue crew arrived and she left the scene, picked up her bicycle and arrived for her night shift covered in blood and oil. She barely mentioned the incident in her next letter home, she buried the pain and shock of what she had witnessed deep inside her. There was nowhere to escape the horror of war. Even on leave in Brighton on one occasion, an enemy plane machine gunned the street she was walking along, sending everyone diving for cover and flattening themselves on the ground, with bullets landing all around them. She said this was a most terrifying experience.

Meanwhile Maurice was now based in the thick of the jungle near Calcutta, enduring spells in hospital with dysentery when he was not in the field. He had not had any leave for more than a year. Eventually, he was granted a month's leave and he travelled to visit friends in Bangalore. On his return he was transferred to a unit in Burma where he was to spend the rest of his serving time. His tour of duty was for three years after which he would be granted home leave. Until then, he and Joan were destined to be apart.

Back in England, Joan had to find somewhere else to live as the family she was staying with had to move house. Finding no suitable alternative accommodation, she had no option but to return to camp. She did not relish the idea especially when she saw her first billet: a room once used as a kitchen, with her bed next to the stove, windows boarded up, a concrete floor and no heating. But in true style, she dismissed the reality of the Spartan appearance of her new accommodation and focused on how she spent her days to cover up her true feelings of despair.

It took Ambrose nearly a year to find a suitable job and in November 1944, he was appointed to the British Consul in Santos, Brazil. In April 1945, he left England to take up his position. He returned to Buenos Aires to be reunited with Lillian before relocating to Santos to begin their new life in the Diplomatic Service.

The war in Europe finally ended in May 1945. Duties prevented Joan from joining the thousands of people celebrating in the Mall and she missed the King and Queen appearing on the balcony of Buckingham Palace. She wrote home with joy describing the feeling of euphoria and elation that came from the relief of the war being over. With the thought of repatriation uppermost in her mind she had the option of returning to Argentina as soon as she was demobilised, or waiting for Maurice to return to England and travel back together. Paddy was the first of the brothers to be demobilised and he and Suzanne were soon on a boat back to Argentina.

As much as she wanted to return home as soon as possible, Joan chose to wait for Maurice so they could return together. Once she was demobilised, she went to live with her aunts in Hove. She expressed her joy of being out of uniform and in her own clothes again, with no one to answer to and no one to dictate her life. The freedom she felt was immense. With time on her hands, she volunteered at the Children's Hospital in Brighton, working in the Outpatients Department where she quickly became a valued member of staff. The Sister said she would have done better training to be a nurse rather than wasting her time as a wireless operator, to which she was inclined to agree. She loved working with the children and longed for the day when she could have a family of her own, something she often referred to in her letters home, especially since both her sisters-in-law had daughters of their own.

Peace may have come to Europe, but the war in the Far East continued on for several months, finally ending in September 1945 with the Japanese surrender. At last Maurice could begin to plan his own repatriation, but this took months to organise. With no firm dates for his return and with her parents now established in Santos, Joan could only dream of the day it would finally happen and they would all be together again. She talked of stopping off in Santos to visit her parents en route to Buenos Aires to have a family reunion. She could hardly wait for the day but, sadly, it never came. Ambrose was taken ill suddenly and she received a telegram from her mother with the news. She was beside herself with worry and berated herself for remaining in England when she had the chance of being repatriated months ago. She begged her mother's forgiveness for not being with her when her father was so ill and not for the first time in her life thought to herself, *Will it always be my lot to constantly be separated from those I love?* Sadly, her father did not recover and he died on 24 March 1946, and was laid to rest in a cemetery in Santos. On hearing the news Viola immediately travelled to Santos to be with her mother and together they returned to Buenos Aires. Lillian was left without means to support herself and would look to her daughters to provide her with a home for the rest of her life. Although Ambrose became wealthy through his expertise as a business manager, once he retired unfortunate, bad investment choices meant he rapidly dissipated his capital.

Eventually, the months of waiting and three years apart came to an end. Joan received the long-awaited telegram from Maurice with news of his arrival, asking her to meet him at the Park Lane Hotel in London on 14 April 1946. Excitedly Joan arrived at the hotel very early and found the place full of RAF personnel waiting to be reunited with their loved ones. She couldn't see Maurice and sat down at a table and began to write a letter home. She was so intent on her writing that she failed to notice Maurice walk passed her, even though she was looking straight at him. They had both changed enough not to be instantly recognizable, especially as Maurice was now tanned and had a bullish moustache. Finally, the months and years of separation were over. Overjoyed to be together again, Joan and Maurice spent a second honeymoon at a cottage belonging to a friend in Ramsbury, the home of her father's family as they waited to hear about their return passage to Buenos Aires. Eventually news came through that they were booked on the SS Loch Monar, sailing from Liverpool on 2 July 1946. At last they were going home!

It was with deep sadness that Alex and Sealy said goodbye to Joan and Maurice as they said farewell to the family who had come to mean so much to them during the last few years. They would especially miss Joan and her lively presence, which had become such a central part of their lives. With their advancing years, they may have wondered if they would ever meet again. My mother never forgot their kindness nor that of her cousins who welcomed her into their home and supported her during her years in voluntary service.

My parents never talked about their war-time experiences. It was as if that part of their lives was locked away and did not need to be brought into the light again. Whatever trauma they experienced, they kept to themselves. Only as my mother's life was drawing to a close did the cracks begin to open as memories started to emerge and the emotional horror of what she had been through finally came to the surface. It was then she showed me the bundle of letters she had written to her family, which my grandmother had kept so carefully all those years, too many memories to throw away. Reading those letters gave me insight into those dark years, the unspoken pain of separation, the heartbreak of being away from her loved ones and the longing to return to her beloved homeland where she could find peace. It is only because of her meticulous attention to detail and numbering each letter she wrote to her family that there is an ongoing story of what she and my father experienced during the war.

My father kept many papers and documents in a small, brown leather briefcase. Amongst these was a testimonial from his Wing Commander saying he had discharged his duties with enthusiasm, he was well liked as a friend and had never been heard to utter a unkind remark about anyone.

On 6 April 2006, the Ambassador of the Argentine Republic and the Anglo-Argentine Society held a Reception at the Argentine Residence in London to commemorate the Argentine volunteers who fought in the Second World War and those who supported them. I know Mum felt immense gratitude that all the volunteers received recognition from the Argentine community. The Reception was combined with the showing of a documentary film *"The Argentine Volunteers in the RAF"* made by Claudio Meunier to launch a book he wrote with Oscar Rimondi called *Alas de Trueno (Wings of Thunder)*. The book is the story of the Anglo-Argentine pilots who joined the Royal Air Force in the Second World War.

(Mr. Meunier is Honour Secretary and official historian of the Association of RAF Argentine veterans).

CHAPTER 8

HOME AGAIN

Joan and Maurice arrived back in Buenos Aires to the loving embrace of
their family, so happy to be home, even though their joy was tinged with
sadness because both their fathers had died during the years they were
away. Ambrose a few months before and Gerald, who passed away in 1944.
Maud was now living with Ged at the Estancia Santa Isabel, near Ortondo,
Venado Tuerto in the Province of Santa Fe. Life had changed for them all.

Their priority was to find somewhere to live and thoughts of starting
a family uppermost in their minds. They chose Hurlingham, a suburb of
Buenos Aires about an hour from the city centre, which had become the
home of many Anglo-Argentines and other Europeans and where Viola
and Frank had already bought a house. Hurlingham developed around
the Hurlingham Club, which was established in 1888 by the local Anglo-
Argentine community and named after the Hurlingham Club in London.
The Club offered sports and social activities, including tennis, squash,
swimming, cricket, golf and polo. Polo was first played in Argentina at
the Hurlingham Club and it was here the Argentine Polo Association was
founded in 1922.

Joan and Maurice found a house to rent near Hurlingham station,
convenient for Maurice's commute to the centre of Buenos Aires when

he returned to work for the River Plate Trust & Company. Renting was only a temporary option, however because they wanted to buy a plot of land and build their own house. They searched for the ideal location and Joan started to design the house with her talent for drawing coming into its own. They found a suitable plot on Isabel la Catolica, an earth road surrounded by open fields. Building had begun when their son, David, was born in December 1947. Eighteen months later, I joined the family, rather traumatically for my parents who thought my birth would take place in the taxi taking them to the British Hospital in the centre of Buenos Aires, an hour's drive from Hurlingham. They had to cross the railway line and the barrier was down for the night and the keeper asleep in his gatehouse. My father had to shout to wake him up and raise the barrier. Fortunately, he managed to rouse the gatekeeper and they made it to the hospital in time for my arrival at dawn on a mid-winter day in June 1949.

Building work on the house took far longer than expected and we continued to live in our rented house. This was not without incident and one night the open fire used to heat the house ignited the wooden joist beneath the floor, causing smoke and flames to erupt. Luckily, the fire was quickly put out before the house was badly damaged. We moved into our new house when I was around two years old. Lillian, who had been living with Viola and Frank since Ambrose had died, came to live with us and became a part of our family.

The designs and drawings of the house were among the treasures I found in a chest of drawers in my mother's attic when we were clearing her house. I had never seen them before and they must have meant a great deal to her and one of the possessions she could never threw away. I looked through the drawings of the house that also came to mean so much to me and remembered the red brick bungalow with its red tiled roof, the porch and entrance hall that led to the passage and the four bedrooms and two bathrooms. The living room led off the hallway into the dining room, separated by sliding doors. The door into the kitchen, utility area, maid's room and bathroom and a small room, which my mother used as her den and workroom. Another door led into the integral garage and back porch where the milkman used to leave the milk in cans.

Our house in Hurlingham

The house was surrounded by a large garden landscaped with trees, bushes, roses and flowerbeds, as well as an area for growing vegetables. The climate encouraged rapid growth of trees and plants and within a few years the garden was well established. I loved the house and have many happy memories of playing in the garden. We strung hammocks under the graceful willow trees, which provided a canopy to keep us cool in the hot summer sun. At the back of the house another tall willow tree held our swing, safe in its strong branches. It grew so fast its roots penetrated under the foundations of the house and came up through the drain hole in the bathroom. I remember looking at its white roots waving like fingers from the darkness of the drain. Sadly the tree had to be cut down. Outside the front of the house was a mulberry tree, which was our favourite tree to climb. It gave delicious tasting berries in the summer and the fallen fruit covered the grass in a deep purple, which ended up as jam that my mother made.

My mother and grandmother, who David and I called Guggy, kept the garden tidy helped by a gardener. Standard roses bordered the path from the garden gate like soldiers guarding the entrance to our home. Large shrubs in every corner provided a haven for our dens and colourful flowers filled the flower beds. We spent many hours in make-believe games and formed the Secret Seven Club with friends who lived nearby. We had no television, computers, i-pads, tablets or electronic games to distract us from the joy of being in nature's outdoor playground.

The house was on a dirt road which created clouds of dust in the dry winter and mud up to our ankles in the summer when the rainy season brought heavy rain and storms and the road became a mud bath and source of entertainment. We had great fun squelching through the mud in wellingtons and watching cars sliding and getting stuck in the mud, as did the horse and cart that delivered the bread and milk in a large churn, which turned sour in stormy weather.

We didn't own a car and bicycles were our only means of transport. Until David and I were old enough to ride our own bicycles, mum took us around on her bicycle with David in a seat on the front and me strapped in a seat on the back and the shopping hung across the back wheel. Once I remember she had bought a bag of cement and carried it home on the back of her bicycle, the front wheels reared up like a horse as she tried to control the weight.

We kept a menagerie of pets, including cats, dogs, budgies and canaries. The budgies came from a market stall by the station in town and dad used to bring them back for us in a brown paper bag. Their home was a large cage on a stand, which went outside every day in the shade of the mulberry tree. One day the wind got up unexpectedly, the cage blew over and the budgies flew away. We saw them in the tree but of course could do nothing about catching and enticing them back to their metal home. They revelled in their newfound freedom of flight and space. Dad bought us some more, carrying them home carefully in the paper bag. This happened often, some died, some flew away and new ones arrived.

We had a beautiful grey cat from our neighbour, Chubby Ford, who bred cats. We called him Tiggy, his fur was long and thick and his fluffy tail stood upright. He was so special. He used to listen for the sound of mum's bicycle as she rode home down the road and always raced to greet her as she came in the gate. One day Tiggy disappeared and never came back. We grieved the loss of our beautiful cat, so Tiggy Two came to live with us and remained a faithful friend.

We also had a black cocker spaniel called Kimmy who was jealous and protective of mum and guarded her fiercely if anyone approached as I found out when I climbed onto her back while she was gardening. Most people kept dogs for protection and whenever we rode our bicycles down the road, stray dogs appeared from nowhere, yapping and barking at our heels as we peddled faster and faster to get away. They were very aggressive and did the same to any car driving passed. We had Kimmy for a number of years and after he died, we got another dog we named Sputnik after the Russian spaceship, which had launched the first dog, Laika, into space. Around the same time, Viola had a new dog, who she named Laika. Sputty, as he became known, was a lovely little white terrier with brown ears that flopped over his eyes. Sadly, Sputty eventually got distemper and had to be put down. Mum was so upset she said she could never have another dog because the pain of their suffering and losing them was too great.

A swimming pool was added in the garden, a necessity in the intense summer heat. For David and I this was heaven. Swimming whenever we liked afforded us many hours of fun and games on our own or with friends. We learned to swim at a young age, an essential life skill, especially with a pool in the garden. I remember one day standing on the edge of the pool with the young daughter of a couple who were visiting. We had probably been sent into the garden to play while the adults were chatting inside the house. Suddenly the little girl slipped and fell into the pool at the deep end. I instinctively knelt down and grabbed her hand as she disappeared under the water. She could not swim, but fortunately I was able to pull her out and we went back into the house, dripping with water and tears. It didn't occur to me at the time that I had probably saved her life, but I do remember her parents giving me a large bag of sweets to say thank you.

Mum became involved with community life in Hurlingham. She joined the Women's Diocesan Association in Argentina and Eastern South America. It was known as the WDA and was a Society of Church women and other people who united in prayer and worked for the local needs of the Diocese. The Bishop had started the Society in 1910 to unite women in the scattered Chaplaincies of the Diocese and to create in them a greater sense of responsibility towards their home, neighbours, church and nation. The WDA raised money for charities and also ran a thrift shop, which helped fund a new church hall at St Mark's Church. Mum spent many hours at the shop and the money raised built a beautiful new hall after we left Hurlingham.

Apart from her community interests, mum also continued to develop her natural creative talent in craft of every description. The den at the back of the house became her haven of creative expression, where she made many exciting and different toys, bags, calendars, picture frames and wooden jigsaw puzzles. She cut out pictures from magazines and stuck them onto plywood cutting out tiny shapes with a fretsaw. She also drew and painted pictures, some of which she framed and made into trays and sold through a major department store in Buenos Aires, which became a popular wedding gift. She also knitted and sewed a variety of toys and other items for the annual Church fete, which was held under the trees at the Hurlingham Club every summer. Mum and Viola had a stand together filled with all the items they had knitted, sewed and crafted. Dad was also involved in the community and became a verger at St Mark's Church. Our social life was centred around the Hurlingham Club, meeting friends, playing tennis, watching cricket and polo and spending time at the pool in the summer.

We travelled to England in May 1954 on home leave sailing from Buenos Aires on the SS Andes. The voyage took three weeks and everyone dressed up for the customary fancy dress party as the ship crossed the Equator. Mum made David and I costumes of Red Indians and asked the chef for some dry pasta shells which she painted red and we wore as necklaces. I remember David fell into the swimming pool and mum dived in to rescue him fully clothed. She lost her watch in the process but saved her son's life, although David has strong memories that he could swim well enough to manage, but was naturally grateful to mum for coming to his rescue.

We arrived in Southampton a week before my fifth birthday and were met by Bobby who was now living and working in London. Together we took the boat train to London before moving down to Hove where we stayed in a boarding house near to the aunts. Sadly, Aunt Sealy had passed away a few months before our arrival. We met Aunt Alex and another Aunt who lived in Earls Court in London and the cousins Mum had stayed with during the war. My parents hired a car and we spent several weeks driving around the country visiting friends and family. We drove up to Scotland, back through the Lake District and Wales connecting with the Brownrigg ancestral roots in Scotland and Cumbria. Meeting up with family and friends must have been a rich and rewarding experience for my parents and a sharp contrast to the last time they had been in England. It was a happy time for us all   We returned to Argentina in October and life continued to unfold. David became a boarder at St Albans College in Lomas de Zamora, and I went to a kindergarten called Tanglewood and had private lessons with a series of governesses, including my cousin, Diana, Viola and Frank's daughter. I started as a daygirl at St Hilda's College when I was eight years old and made many lifelong friends, many of whom I am in touch with to this day.

Holidays were spent with Uncle Ged at the Estancia Santa Isabel and later Estancia Santa Emelia in Venado Tuerto, in the Province of Santa Fe. We travelled there by car borrowed from Viola and Frank, who had a habit of naming their cars, one was Rebecca and a later one Jezebel. No matter which direction we travelled, the tarmac roads took us only so far until we had to turn off down earth roads. These roads seemed endless and as it inevitably rained, we usually got stuck in the mud and sometimes needed rescuing. The rain also meant the canvas roof of the car leaked and we had to hold up our picnic cups to catch the water. Our journeys were always eventful! Despite the journey, I loved staying in the camp at the *estancias*, and the uplifting and distinctive smell of the eucalyptus trees, the sounds of the birds, *asados* under the trees and riding across the wide open fields are my happiest memories of our life in Argentina. I learned to ride at a young age. As an experienced rider, mum was keen to pass on her passion, which she certainly did. I loved riding as much as she did and found a sense of freedom galloping across the wide, open spaces of the flat *pampas*.

We also had holidays at the seaside in the summer, staying at the seaside resorts of Chapadmalal, Miramar and Mar del Plata with Viola and Frank, renting houses together and enjoying the wide sandy beaches stretching for mile after mile, sand dunes and cliffs to climb and safe swimming in ocean waves. It was ideal for children and adults alike. Often we combined a seaside holiday with visiting friends at nearby *estancias*. On one such occasion, it began to rain and the roads became impassable. We had to spend the night in a hotel. No star ratings, we were lucky enough to find a bed for the night, but the sheets were dirty, cockroaches all over the floor. Mum wouldn't let us lie on the beds until she had put towels over the bedding. A night we never forgot!

CHAPTER 9

LIFE CHANGES

We were happy living in Hurlingham and loved the lifestyle Argentina offered. However, there was growing unease about the future in Argentina due to the political unrest, which resulted in frequent revolutions and military coups. Although too young to understand politics, I have memories of tanks rolling down the main street and the sound of gunfire. We lived near an army base and whenever the government failed, the military took over until a new president was elected and the process started again. The undercurrent of unrest created instability for the future and coincided with my father facing the loss of his job when his company decided to close down. He was 57 years old and knew it would not be easy to find another job in the current state of uncertainty. My parents were also concerned about our education. I was happy and doing well at St Hilda's College but David was struggling at his school and they needed another option. The fees at St George's College were beyond their financial reach and they did not want to send David to boarding school in England because of their own unhappy memories of being sent away to school. The writing was on the wall and with great reluctance they took the heart-breaking decision that it was time for us to leave Argentina and look for a better life in England. The house went on the market, most of our possessions were sold or given away to friends and the rest packed into crates to take with us.

Our passage to England was booked on the SS Duquesa, leaving on 6 February 1960. We had a farewell party for our friends and a final holiday with Uncle Ged to say goodbye to him and our friends in the camp. The sale of our house went through and while our parents did the final packing, David and I went to stay with the MacIver's at Estancia La Esperanza near San Clemente. Heather MacIver and I were born within a week of each other and introduced as playmates when we were five years old when Heather came to live in Hurlingham with her Aunty Chubby, two doors from our house on Isabel la Catolica. We had become firm friends and spent most days playing in each other's houses. I knew how much I was going to miss her and was looking forward to spending time together before we left.

Mum and dad were to join us after the sale of the house was completed. I cannot imagine what they must have felt as they handed the keys to the new owners and left their beloved home for the last time. Even though they sold the house to friends, which may have helped ease their pain, their hearts must have been breaking as their car journey to La Esperanza showed. They left Hurlingham for the four-hour drive to the camp and were expected to arrive late afternoon. David and I, Heather and her brother, Donny, saddled our horses and waited in the *monte,* the small wooded area between the house and the road, intending to ride out and greet them on their arrival. We waited and waited, but they didn't come. Eventually, it became dark and we returned to the house.

Next morning, we woke to find mum and dad had arrived in the middle of the night after an eventful journey. Their car had broken down with a punctured tyre and a broken fan belt, which dad managed to fix using one of mum's stockings. The engine continued to overheat and they had to keep stopping for it to cool down and find water to fill the radiator. They had packed a picnic of sandwiches and drinks, but not expecting a long journey had run out of provisions. Once they left the main road and entered the wilderness of the camp, they were on their own. Desperate for water to fill the radiator, they drove slowly with windows open listening for the sound of frogs to lead them to water. Once located, dad carried water back to the car in mum's shower cap. Their journey took them more than 14 hours and they must have wondered if they would ever make it. When they finally reached the gate of La Esperanza, the car died completely and they had to push it off the road and walk up the drive to the house. It wasn't a great distance, but through the *monte* with only owls and moonlight for guidance and dogs on the alert for intruders, it must have seemed never-ending. Certainly it was a journey they never forgot and ever since then, mum always had a thermos of tea, water and biscuits in a basket in the back of the car so she would never have to go through that experience again. We stayed at La Esperanza enjoying time with dear friends, until the moment came for our departure. The car had been fixed and it was time to leave. It was an emotional farewell and Heather and I promised to write to each other and keep in touch.

Our journey back to Hurlingham was uneventful and a few days later we stood on deck of the SS Duquesa saying goodbye our family and friends and the land we loved so dear.

Joan and Maurice with David and Jeanine leaving Argentina
6 February 1960

We waved goodbye as our ship pulled away from the quayside and we left Argentina, setting sail across the ocean to return to the land of our ancestors. When, or even if, we would return to Argentina was not in our minds. We were probably numb with the shock and reality of what we were doing. It may have been a conscious choice based on logical and sound reasons, but the mind has a way of convincing the heart it knows best. All I remember is the sadness I felt, and I expect my parents felt the same way I did. I cannot imagine they wanted to leave our beautiful house, family, friends and homeland for a new life in England but they probably felt it was their only choice. There would be no going back, we could only look ahead and see where our path would take us.

I was too young to understand the sacrifice they were making to leave a home which meant so much to us all, in the hope that England would provide a better and more stable future. The soul searching, which must have taken place was never something David and I knew about and neither of us remembered talking about the underlying reasons for our departure. It is only with maturity and reflection that we have seen how pulling up our roots and leaving took immense courage. As children we didn't understand the consequences of what a new life in England would entail, despite the fact that we were told we were 'going home.' All I knew was we were leaving the only home I had known and the land we loved so dearly and it affected us far more deeply that we realised.

CHAPTER 10

A NEW LIFE IN ENGLAND

Our voyage across the Atlantic Ocean took three weeks. The SS Duquesa was a small commercial cargo ship, which carried 12 passengers and called at Montevideo in Uruguay and St Vincent, in the Cape Verde Islands. Some of the passengers left in Montevideo and we virtually had the ship to ourselves. It was our private ocean liner, with a cabin each and meals at the Captain's table. The crew put up a small canvas pool for our use and we had the run of the ship, including the Bridge.

We left Argentina at the height of a southern-hemisphere summer and arrived in England in the depths of a northern-hemisphere winter. The contrast couldn't have been more extreme. As our ship crossed the Bay of Biscay with huge waves surging over the bow, grey clouds, strong winds, lashing rain and freezing cold we had a taste of the weather to expect in our new homeland. We sailed up the English Channel with a certain amount of trepidation, as well as anticipation and excitement as we focused on where our life was taking us on our new adventure.

Our ship docked at Tilbury on 27 February 1960 on a cold, grey winter's day. Once again, Bobby was there to meet us and accompany us on the boat train into London. Our worldly possessions were eventually offloaded into storage until we had somewhere to live. Bobby had booked us into a boarding house in Marylebone where we stayed for the first few weeks. I can remember the house was newly refurbished and had a smell of paint. Our first morning we went shopping for winter clothes and before long we came down with coughs and colds, unaccustomed to the cold English weather.

Once we had settled in and began to feel better, the next priority was to buy a car so mum and dad could begin driving round the countryside looking for somewhere to live. Meanwhile, David and I were left under the care of our cousin Diana, who had a flat in Earls Court. They knew their only option was to be self-employed and were looking for a business premises with a family house attached. Mum had high standards and nothing they saw came up to their requirements. With the search taking longer than planned, we left Marylebone and moved into a flat in Ealing, opposite the Common. David started school as a boarder at Fernden, the family prep school in Haslemere where the Brownrigg boys had attended. My school fate awaited me because this was dependent on where we lived.

Eventually, and possibly in slight desperation, mum and dad chose to rent a house in Ashtead, Surrey as Viola and Frank were on their way to England with Guggy, who was returning to live with us and we needed a home quickly. Shortly after renting the house, however, they found a suitable business in Horsham, West Sussex, with a general store and post office, which they liked well enough to make an offer. The property also had a two-bedroom apartment above the premises, which they saw as providing additional income. A sound idea, except the business had a bakery attached and the bakers started work at four o'clock in the morning. They needed to employ a member of staff to let them in and this person had to live in the flat. Neither mum nor dad had ever worked in retail before, let alone run a business. Dad took on responsibility for the post office and the accounts, while mum was in charge of the shop and the staff employed in the shop and bakery. The business was 40 minutes from Ashtead, which meant they needed to buy a second car. Money was rolling out of their pockets like water and their dreams appeared to be falling apart. The reality of what they had taken on board became a steep learning curve, leaving them wondering why their decision to leave Argentina had felt so right.

There was, however, a suitable girl's school conveniently located down the road from our house in Ashtead, where I was duly enrolled to begin in the summer term. Except, I was ill at the start of the term and did not begin until after the term had begun, which was not an easy experience. Once we moved into our new house and Guggy had arrived, our new life began. With mum and dad leaving early to open the shop and not returning till evening, Guggy became my surrogate mother and with David away at boarding school, I felt the emotional insecurity of being in unfamiliar territory, missing mum and dad and my friends and finding it hard to settle in my new school.

Those first few months saw us all having to adjust to our new life and new environment with smaller houses and pocket-sized gardens, to say nothing of the English weather. Mum and dad had to get used to running a business, managing staff and a bakery, greeting customers, working with a new currency and driving on the left side of the road instead of the right. Somehow we managed to keep smiling and find time to relax amid all the changes and hard work. One of the first places we went to was the seaside at West Wittering in West Sussex, recommended by a member of staff who worked in the shop. We found our way to the glorious sandy beach on the south coast at the entrance to Chichester Harbour, where we spent many wonderful days having picnics and enjoying the seaside, little realising we would live nearby one day.

Life continued to unfold over the next two years as we settled into a routine and gradually began to feel more at home in our new surroundings. I remember the first time it snowed and we woke to a winter wonderland. Something I had never seen before, which was pure magic! However, more than magic was needed for my parents who had to commute to Horsham every day, manage a home and business and survive in a new land. They realised that living and working in different locations was not economically viable in the long term and decided it was time to find somewhere else to live with fewer overheads. The experience gained during the last two years helped them prioritise the importance of needing a large family house with a business attached, preferably without a post office and bakery, neither of which they had found conducive to their sanity and wellbeing.

They searched the property market again and saw an advert describing; *'An Olde Worlde Village Stores near Chichester, general grocer and off-licence. Delightful premises with five beds. Business established more than 100 years. Four acres of land with outbuildings. Ideal for family wanting to run chickens, pigs, market garden.'* I am not sure they had a market garden with chickens and pigs in mind, but it seemed the large family house combined with a general store with extensive grounds was an answer to their prayers. The property was located in Birdham, a village about five miles south of Chichester and a short distance from the beach at West Wittering. They rang the agents, visited the property, fell in love with it and put in an offer. The family agreed to share costs which made it a viable proposition. The business in Horsham was sold, the house in Ashtead vacated and I left my school down the road. I was enrolled for boarding school at Oak Hall in Haslemere, Surrey, where a number of Argentine friends had sent their daughters. My parents hoped I would feel more settled at Oak Hall than I had at my first school, *déja vu* with mum's parents having the same idea when they sent her to school in England. David was also moving onto public school in East Sussex. A new chapter in our lives was about to begin for us all.

CHAPTER 11

EARNLEYS

We moved to Birdham in the summer of 1962. Our Olde Worlde village stores was named Earnleys, after a nearby hamlet. The original property with thatched roof dated back around 300 years and had been extensively rebuilt in 1875 with flint and brick and the shop had become integral to the main house. The property was approached by a wide gravel drive leading to a number of outhouses, including a garage, barn and smoking shed. One end of the barn had been converted into a small studio and a one bedroom flat had been built above the garage. The main house had been extended from the original small cottage, which left the ceiling of the kitchen considerably lower than the rest of the house. Above the kitchen was another small self-contained flat, accessed via the back stairs from the kitchen, which could also be reached through a cupboard in a bedroom in the main house. The house and shop area needed refurbishing and redecorating, including new plumbing, electrical wiring and a central heating system installed. A large garden ran beside the house and extended along the back of adjoining properties to a field overlooking farmland. The spaciousness we had all missed had been found. My parents saw its potential, not only as a family home and business, but also providing additional income from renting the separate accommodation.

We spent our first summer at Earnleys getting used to our new surroundings, decorating rooms sanding floors, painting walls and maintaining the garden. The shop was open throughout the upheaval which was a challenge in itself. We loved the space our new home afforded us, as well as being in a rural area rather than in the middle of a town. Best of all was the beautiful beach at West Wittering, now only a short distance away, where we could escape to after a long day. It seemed too good to be true. We were all happier and more relaxed and the financial burden had been lifted off my parents' shoulders. They cut back on the expense of a second car and the time and cost in travelling to and from home and business, and were able to focus on the future with a degree of confidence, which had not been with them since we first arrived in England. My mother indulged in her love of gardening when time allowed and Guggy enjoyed tending the roses. David and I felt at home in a large garden with plenty of trees to climb. We grew our own vegetables, ably assisted by a gardener, who helped around the property doing the odd jobs, always willing to do whatever was asked of him. He had the broadest of Sussex accents and at times was quite difficult to understand, but he always had a smile on his face and loved his tea and biscuits. He had never been out of the area and coming from Argentina must have seemed like we had arrived from another planet.

The studio at the end of the barn was rented to a talented photographic artist who was stone deaf but able to lip-read and carry on a conversation as though he had perfect hearing. His studio displayed his works of art and photographs he had taken of film stars and celebrities of the day, and over the years he took many portraits of the family. The flat above the garage was refurbished and rented out to a variety of tenants which mum insisted on redecorating between each tenancy. With her attention to detail and desire for perfection, it took days to complete the task and she was never satisfied until it all looked pristine.

With home and business combined, we settled into life on the south coast and began to feel more at peace. Our meals were easily and quickly prepared with a larder on hand which never ran out of food. Guggy helped mum with the cooking and housework as well as the garden. The shop was open every day except for Sundays and half-day on Wednesdays. With a shop on hand, it was easy to come up with refreshments for friends who dropped by and we enjoyed seeing many of our Argentine friends when they were on holiday in England. We continued the Argentine custom of entertaining with many friends together. In the summer, dad used his cooking skills on an *asado,* building the fire in a wheelbarrow, which he moved around the garden according to which way the wind was blowing, in the unpredictable English weather.

Although the shop was closed on Sundays, this did not stop people knocking at the door if they needed something urgently. The most regular Sunday customers were the boys from a local boarding school when they came to spend their pocket money on sweets. Dad always opened the door to them, no matter what time of day. Many customers telephoned for orders and dad did a weekly delivery. Apart from the gardener, a young sales assistant helped them in the shop, serving customers, stacking shelves and making up orders. As well as constantly reordering goods and dealing with paperwork, there was always plenty to do around the house and garden and mum became very adept at Doing It Yourself.

Joan and Maurice outside Earnleys

81

Our first winter in Sussex coincided with the longest and coldest winter in England for more than 200 years. We were celebrating David's birthday with a picnic in the New Forest when the first snowflakes began to fall. We finished eating our sandwiches and set off for home before the snow settled. It kept falling all winter and remained on the ground until the spring. Everything was frozen even the stream, which ran along the back of the property and provided David and I with an unexpected skating rink. While I had the luxury of a warm boarding school, David had to endure cold and draughty passages of his unheated school premises. Our parents and Guggy lived through the winter with kerosene lamps and a coal fire in the sitting room for warmth because the central heating in the house had not yet been installed. Thankfully, the kitchen had an Aga, which gave out some warmth and dad became very attuned to its needs. He stoked the fire with fierce determination and was able to keep it under his firm control as long as the wind did not change direction suddenly, in which case it either went out or roared like a furnace, producing enough heat to boil a kettle in a minute. The uncontrolled temperatures made cooking unpredictable and on one occasion it took about eight hours to roast a chicken! However, standing against the Aga was a wonderful place to keep warm and in this position nothing else mattered. Sometimes the wind made the most extraordinary noise coming through the windows in the living room, which sounded like howling hyenas. Once it was so bad that David went outside to bang the glass to try and stop the noise. The cold weather had made the glass fragile and his banging broke the window and the wind and snow blew into the room with the curtains at 90 degrees. Panic ensued until a large piece of wood was found to secure the window before the room became submerged in snow and ice. Next time the wind howled, we knew better and did our best to ignore the sound.

What with our home renovations, serving in the shop, driving to the Cash and Carry and stocking up shelves, mum was never still for a moment. Constantly on the go as well as her inability to rest caused her body to create enforced time-out and she began to suffer more and more with migraine headaches and sometimes was laid up for hours unable to move. She also suffered from pain in her neck, which she maintained was because of her childhood falls, especially the time she hit the roof of the car when it hit a trench in the road and she heard her neck crack. During the years, she had tried a number of treatments to alleviate the pain, including traction and wearing a surgical collar. It was seeing her with a collar round her neck one day that prompted a customer to tell her about Arthur Johnson, a spiritual healer from East Wittering who she had consulted with great success. Mum was desperate and with memories of the healing experience she had as a child, made an appointment to see him. Arthur was a kind and gentle man and had what he described as x-ray vision, an ability to see into the body and get a deeper understanding of what was going on beneath the pain. Arthur reopened a door into the world of healing for mum, which had enthralled her since she was seven years old. Although, she never said what Arthur told her about her neck problems and migraines, she and dad continued to see him regularly for many years.

Life settled into a routine and we became content with the way things were unfolding, although with a shop to run there was no possibility of going away on holiday. My parents never had another holiday together, whereas David and I were offered a holiday to Spain with Viola and Frank when they came over to England. We jumped at the chance and excitedly flew off to Madrid and from there hired a car and drove to the south, visiting Cordoba, Seville, Granada, and Jerez. We arrived in Malaga when David became unwell and we had to cut short our trip and return home.

At the end of the following year, I had to leave boarding school as the fees became too much for my parents with all the outgoings of running a home and business. I was upset to be leaving as Frances, a friend from St Hilda's had joined the school and it was lovely to have a friend from Argentina. But I had no choice and had to get used to yet another new school. My parents found a local day school near Chichester for me, which worked out well and I completed my O-Level General Certificate of Education examinations and went onto college to do my A-levels.

On 14 February 1966, I arrived home from school to find Guggy had been taken ill suddenly. She had been cleaning the silver when she began to feel unwell and called my mother. She sat down in her chair and within a few minutes she lost consciousness. I arrived home as the ambulance arrived. She was taken to hospital but sadly she died on the way. The cause of her death was an embolism. The shock of her sudden death was devastating, she had been part of our family all my life and we felt her loss deeply. A few months later, Bobby also became ill and needed surgery for a stomach complaint, which turned out to be cancer. He came to convalesce with us at home after the operation, but sadly died shortly afterwards. Bobby never married and spent many weekends with us in Sussex, always joining in for Christmas and other holidays. He was great fun to be with and loved by everyone and we felt his loss so close to Guggy's passing. The house felt empty after they had gone, but life goes on and we had to get used to living without them.

David left his public school after taking his O-Level General Certificate of Education Examinations and enrolled at Chichester College of Further Education (Chichester College of Technology) on a two-year Ordinary National Diploma in Business Studies combined with A-levels. On completion of my GCEs the following year, I joined him at the college to do a similar course with added shorthand and typing skills. David learnt to drive and bought his first car, a green Morris Minor, from money earned doing weekend gardening jobs, and together we drove to college every day.

During our college years, David and I had part-time jobs working at the Chichester Festival Theatre over several seasons, thanks to an introduction by the Manager of the Festival Theatre who was renting the flat. David worked behind the scenes in props and I worked in the front of house, the theatre restaurant and also in the Box Office. On completing his Diploma, David decided to train as an accountant and became articled to a firm in Chichester. I was more undecided at the end of my college days. My desire was to find a way to return to Argentina and achieve that in the quickest way possible. I had an idea of working on a ship, and also considered a career in nursing but in the end opted for the easy route to use my secretarial training and get a job in an office. A friend ran an employment agency in London and found me a suitable position. I was excited at the prospect, however, before I had time to make plans, the position was withdrawn and I had to rethink my options. I found a job locally at Chichester Yacht Basin, working in the New Boat Department of a yacht agency where I stayed for a year or so before deciding to join an airline and move to London. I shared a flat with Argentine friends which was fun but I didn't settle in my job and decided to return home and rethink my future.

As our parents watched David and I become adults, they must have felt they had made the right decision to leave Argentina. Thanks to the sacrifice they had made, we had completed our education, passed our GCEs, obtained Diplomas and were now set on career paths. They seemed content to cut the ties with the past and never spoke about returning to Argentina. In addition, Viola and Frank were planning on leaving Argentina and had bought an apartment in Torremolinos in southern Spain ready for their retirement, which meant they would be nearer and able to visit more often.

David completed his articles and applied for a postgraduate degree at Lancaster University. We waved him goodbye to begin his year's course. A few months later he became engaged to Marion, who he had met through a college friend a year before. They set their wedding date for the end of December and asked me to be a bridesmaid. Exciting news except I was planning my return to Argentina, which had unexpectedly manifested through Viola and Frank, who had generously given me a return ticket to Buenos Aires as a 21st birthday gift. My idea was to spend the summer in Argentina from November to March. However, David and

Marion's impending marriage meant delaying my departure until after their wedding so I put my plans on hold. As it happened, life had other plans for me and despite my heart's longing and best intentions to make it back to Argentina, the time was not yet right for this to happen.

While working for the yacht agency, I had met a guy who worked in an adjoining office and we had been going out for some time. He had recently changed jobs and was relocating to Tokyo. I went to wave him off at the airport and as we said goodbye, he asked me to marry him - his timing could have been better. I said Yes, with my mind trying to work out how I was going to visit Argentina and get married at the same time. An exciting adventure awaited me. I began researching travel options until my fiancé said he could return to England over the New Year holiday when everything shuts down in Tokyo and suggested we get married then. It seemed the obvious answer and I immediately dropped all ideas of my trip to Argentina and began planning our wedding instead. It was mid-December and venues for wedding receptions were booked for Christmas and New Year parties. Eventually I found a nearby hotel willing to host the reception and the vicar of East Wittering was willing to marry us on a Sunday when the venue was available. The date was set four days after David and Marion's wedding. My fiancé flew in from Tokyo and arrived during their wedding reception. There was no time to send out invitations, and we invited family and friends by telephone or chance meetings and had more than 100 guests. As both weddings were held during the New Year holiday, the wedding suits could not be returned immediately so grooms and groomsmen were able to mix and match trousers and jackets. The bridesmaid's dresses worn by our young cousins for both weddings were adapted with a bit of lace. Margaret, my Hurlingham childhood friend, who was now living in England, was my chief bridesmaid and I bought a dress for her to wear. Dad won a premium bond, which paid for my bridal gown which I chose with mum from a local department store.

Somehow, it all came together and within four days, David and I were married and had left home. David and Marion returned to Lancaster and I flew off with my new husband to Tokyo, via New York, San Francisco and Hawaii to a married life on the other side of the world!

CHAPTER 12

A LIFE ALONE

Following the whirlwind of two weddings in a week and the departure of both their children to married life, mum and dad were left to pick up the pieces on their own. The house must have felt extremely quiet and empty after the family and guests left and the excitement died down as they faced another separation from their loved ones. This time they were the ones left behind, rather than the ones who were leaving. Echoing all the times in the past with memories of when they had been parted from their families over the years. At least David was in England and within telephone reach. Whereas, I was on the other side of the world, living in a land few people knew much about, except the part Japan had played during the war. I began writing letters home with news of our new experiences, as my mother had done when she had left home during the war years. I sent colourful postcards capturing the essence of our new homeland and wrote letters twice a week, completely unaware that none of these arrived for more than three months due to a postal strike in England and no-one heard from us from the moment we said goodbye at the airport. From their point of view we completely disappeared.

On reflection, it is hard to imagine how this silence may have affected my parents knowing how they loved to keep in touch with the family. They had to accept the silence as they had done during the war when communication was unreliable and it took weeks for news to travel across the oceans. A different experience to 21st century communication with mobile telephones and the Internet enabling instant connection 24/7 wherever we are in the world. Fifty years ago, communication was primarily through postal services, telephone and telex. With the postal strike taking mail and telephone out of action and with telex used primarily in business, there was no way of keeping in touch with either myself or David and he was only in Lancaster. He said he couldn't even ring home as the phone boxes were jammed with coins. Completely unaware of the silence between us, I continued to write letters and send postcards and, it was not until we had a telephone call from Viola when she arrived in Spain three months later to find out if we were alright did I learn that none of my letters and postcards had reached home.

It was a shock to hear that my parents had not heard a word from us from the moment we had waved goodbye at the airport. There was nothing I could have done but when dad's health began to deteriorate a few months later and he was diagnosed with cancer, I wondered if this final separation affected him deeper than he realised. I felt helpless being so far away and unable to be with him and support mum. Likewise, David and Marion had moved to Barbados and both of us were out of reach. It was left to my mother to look after him, as well as keep the business running, until Viola came to her rescue and moved in to give her support.

We returned from Tokyo on leave eighteen months after we had left. We stayed with mum and dad at Earnleys and it was lovely to be back and meet up with our families and friends again. We cherished our time together especially with focus on my father's illness. I could tell the additional stress mum was under and sadly his health deteriorated and one morning he woke unable to move his legs. He was admitted to hospital and investigations found secondary tumours had caused his spine to collapse leaving him paralysed. He spent many weeks in hospital until he was able to be discharged home. Mum converted a ground-floor room into his bedroom and was supplied with a hospital bed and a pressure relieving mattress and a hoist to aid his care.

Mum continued to look after dad and the shop as best she could, but eventually she could not keep the business running on her own and the shop closed. Another chapter ended and mum felt the relief of simplifying her life. She became my father's constant companion and full-time carer. At that time, community support services were not as well established as they are now and she had to employ a nurse to look after him for a few hours once a week to give herself some time off. She devoted herself to his needs using the nursing skills she had learnt during her volunteer work in hospitals when she was younger. When the weather was good, she took dad into the garden in a wheelchair to enjoy the fresh air and sunshine. The rest of the time he spent in his room and loved nothing more than mum reading to him. She said not once during his illness did he ever complain. He seemed able to accept his condition without a murmur, though he must have spent many long hours wondering why this had happened to him. He was simply grateful and appreciative for the care he received, not only from his beloved wife, but also the doctors and nurses who did their best to make him comfortable. We stayed at Earnleys for several months until we had to return. Another goodbye. It never got any easier, more so now leaving dad in his condition and mum coping on her own.

Eighteen months later, I returned to England heavily pregnant with my first child and stayed with mum and dad at Earnleys once again. My husband followed a few weeks later and arrived in time for the birth of our beautiful baby boy. We spent the first few weeks with mum and dad which gave them time to get to know their first grandson and later we moved into our bungalow nearby, which we had bought on our first trip home. My husband returned to Japan and I went to stay with mum and dad until the time came for me to leave. I knew I couldn't stay forever and with a heavy heart, I returned to Tokyo with our son who was five months old. I didn't want to think about whether or not I would see dad again.

Life carried on until I had a telephone call from mum saying dad had peacefully passed into spirit. It was a shock to hear the sad news, even though in my heart I knew he was dying. I felt relief that his suffering was over but the reality of death hits hard. Within a few days, I was on the plane to London with our 15 month old son. Many times since I have wondered why I did not return sooner to spend more time with dad, yet maybe it is not what either of us truly wanted. It is only now I realise that my mother faced the same dilemma with her father when he became ill. She could have returned to see her father as I could have returned to see mine. We both have regrets but have to accept the choices we made. were for the best.

Dad's funeral took place a few days later and we said goodbye to a wonderful, kind and generous man who never had a cross word to say about anyone. I loved him deeply. He was a loving and supportive father and I am truly blessed he was my dad. Mum seemed at peace, thankful that her beloved's suffering had ended. She said she felt a void within her, missing his physical presence but also felt surrounded by a bubble of love, which helped her through the difficult times. Once more she had to adjust to life without him, as she had done when they had been separated during the war. At least then, she had hope in her heart of the day they would be together again, now all she had were the memories and the love they had shared.

After the funeral, we took ourselves off in the car, visiting friends to get away and enjoy the summer weather. David and Marion had returned from overseas and now had a son of their own. The next generation was arriving and I am sure my father was happy to have met his two grandsons. I know he would have been a wonderful grandfather in the same way he had been a wonderful father and role model to his children.

After a few weeks, I returned to Japan, my heart was heavy with grief of losing my father and leaving my mother on her own. Living on the other side of the world was not easy and a few months later we decided to leave Japan and return to England. Naturally, mum was delighted with our decision and we stayed with her when we first arrived before moving into our bungalow once the tenants had left. I was pregnant again and we needed a larger house for our growing family. We sold our bungalow and found a modern four-bedroom house in West Wittering. We stayed with mum before completing the purchase of our new house and were still with her when our beautiful second son was born, the day before my birthday. Like his older brother, he spent the first few weeks of his life under the watchful eye of his grandmother.

My mother enjoyed our company while we waited to move into our new house. Earnleys was a large house for one person, but mum seemed happy to stay there and continued to rent the flats to increase her income. We were a distraction for her and she loved nothing more than getting to know her grandchildren. The shop area had been converted into a living room and provided a play area for the boys as they grew up. The large floor space became a roller skating track or indoor football ground, affording plenty of room for the riotous and noisy games boys love to play. The garden had plenty of trees to climb and open space for the children to run around in and we enjoyed many happy times together.

As much as mum loved living at Earnleys, it was uneconomical for her to continue living in such a large property and with a financial gift from her sister, mum began to look for a smaller house for herself. After a lot of house hunting for her perfect home, which once again was proving hard to find, she eventually settled for a small semi-detached house in Felpham. Twenty years of accumulated possessions had to be sorted and another house sale took place. Memories of leaving Hurlingham must have been uppermost in her mind as she sorted out what to take and what she no longer needed. With our help the house was cleared, the property sold and she moved the few miles to Felpham. Not as far as she had moved previously, but in a different direction which meant she did not have to pass her old home every day.

Another chapter began for mum which she found challenging to some degree. She found it hard adjusting to a small semi-detached house, with a pocket-handkerchief garden in a cul-de-sac surrounded by other people. She was used to a large detached house and garden with no immediate neighbours and did not like being overlooked. She planted a high hedge in the front garden for privacy and shrubs in the back garden. The house was compact, easy to heat and economical to run, all the reasons why it was a good choice, except she found it small and cramped after Earnleys and the other houses she had lived in. In the end she accepted the advantages of a modern house that could easily be locked up when she went away and acknowledged it would take time to adjust to her new space.

With time on her hands, she was able to go away on holiday for the first time since leaving Argentina and made frequent trips to visit Viola and Frank in Spain. It was on one of these visits she told us about a strange experience. One afternoon, she was walking down the hill after a trip into town and saw three large dark clouds in an otherwise cloudless blue sky, which, to her eyes, resembled unidentified flying craft. She stopped in amazement at the sight, looking around to see if anyone else had seen what she had seen, only to find herself totally alone with not a soul in sight. As she said, this in itself was very unusual because in the height of summer there are always plenty of people walking about the streets. She returned to the apartment speechless and puzzled. No reports in the papers or radio broadcasts mentioned anything unusual that day, but it remained a very strong impression in her memory. It reminded her of a dream she used to have as a child of going outside and looking up at the night sky and seeing a huge ship above her head. She never felt afraid and had an overwhelming sense of peace.

Mum loved her trips to Spain, spending time with Frank and Viola and the opportunity of speaking Spanish again. They travelled around the area visiting Gibraltar and Morocco enjoying the warmth of the Mediterranean climate. We likewise enjoyed their hospitality spending summer holidays at their apartment complex, which provided the perfect resort for families and children with easy access to the beach and swimming pools. It was a holiday paradise. Our family was growing, David and Marion had three boys and we had a beautiful daughter to complete our family. Mum adored her grandchildren and they adored their grandmother, or Nana as they called her. My mother rekindled her love of knitting, returning from her holidays with identical jumpers for each of her grandchildren. She had an ability to read and knit at the same time and thus spent many hours peacefully occupied.

Within another few years, we also moved house. As much as we liked the house in West Wittering, the garden was too small for the children as they grew up. We searched around and eventually found a 1930s Edwardian house nearby with two acres of land. The property was in need of restoration and the large garden resembled an enchanted forest covered in thick brambles. The house needed a complete renovation, which made it impossible to live there and mum offered to have us stay with her while the building work took place. It was rather a squash but I am sure mum loved having us around. We moved in as soon as our new home was habitable and mum was a great help with decorating. She spent hours stripping the staircase covered in brown paint and revealed a beautiful pine staircase, a rich reward for all her hard work.

CHAPTER 13

NEW BEGINNINGS

In the ten years since dad died, mum took up new interests and joined a number of local groups. She gradually found a social life for herself, something she never had time for while my father was alive and they had a shop to run. She kept in touch with many friends from Argentina who had returned to live in England. On one level of her being, however, she was still looking to find a way to fulfil her passion for healing, which had been with her since the powerful experience she had when she was a child. Now, in her mid-60s, with no obligations or responsibilities to anyone apart from herself and no one to tell her what she could or could not do, the doorway to her healing path began to open.

Over the years, she continued to visit Arthur and loved talking to him and his wife, Mon, about the world of spirit and healing. Mon and Arthur introduced her to COMPASS, the Chichester Open Meeting for Psychical and Spiritual Studies, where she met Pat Herington who told her about Touch for Health, a self-help technique she had read about in a magazine and used to relieve her recurring back problem. Touch for Health was developed by Dr John Thie, a chiropractor from California, USA, who had worked with a fellow chiropractor, George Goodhart, who introduced Applied Kinesiology to his work in the 1970s. Applied Kinesiology used muscle testing biofeedback to identify imbalances in the meridian energy system in the body which can be released by holding specific points on the body to restore a state of balance. John Thie simplified his technique and called it Touch for Health, to enable ordinary people to help themselves, their families and friends.

Pat had ordered a manual and asked her husband to follow the simple instructions for healing back pain while she lay on the bed. After several sessions over the course of a few days, Pat was astonished to find her back pain had gone. Amazed at her remarkable recovery, she wrote to John Thie who put her in touch with Brian Butler, who was responsible for bringing Touch for Health to the United Kingdom. Pat signed up for the training with Brian Butler and became an Instructor in 1984.

My mother was enthused by Pat's story and wanted to learn more about Touch for Health and signed up for an Introductory Course with her in May 1986. The technique captivated her and she signed up for the Instructor Training with Brian Butler and became a qualified Instructor in August 1986.

Although mum had a basic understanding of human anatomy and had worked in hospitals, Touch for Health took her into a deeper world as she learned about the life force energy which flows through the human body along energy pathways called meridians. This life force energy is known in different cultures and traditions as prana, ki, or chi. Blockages in the meridians build up through negative thoughts, emotions and patterns of behaviour, which stops the chi from flowing freely. Over a period of time this results in imbalances in the human body, which eventually can lead to ill health and disease. Muscle testing helps to identify where the imbalances lie and, using specific techniques, these can be released to allow energy to flow freely once more and restore the body to its natural state of balance.

Enthusiasm in my mother and her Touch for Health friends quickly spread and they began meeting regularly to exchange knowledge and treatments. Their treatments became known as a Balance. Soon, they decided to formalise their work and spread it to a wider audience and started a newsletter with articles about Touch for Health and other related topics and dates of meetings. One of the founder members, Maureen Hardy, undertook the role of Editor and The Balance Sheet was born.

In the spring of 1987, a Touch for Health promotion day was organised and a room at the local library booked for the event. My mother and her friends were not sure what response to expect from the public and they took their couches and knitting in case no one turned up! However, a local journalist had recently experienced a Balance and wrote an enthusiastic article about Touch for Health in the Complementary Therapy section of the local newspaper, giving the date of the promotion where free Balances would be on offer. On the day of the event, my mother and her colleagues arrived at the library and were astonished to find people already queuing. So many people turned up that their original idea of giving individual Balances was quickly changed to an introductory talk and demonstrations. The room could only accommodate a certain number and they had to allow people in, group by group to prevent overcrowding. By the end of the day they had spoken to over 200 people!

Clearly, the enthusiastic response that Touch for Health was receiving indicated it was time for expansion. A suitable venue was needed where they could meet and see clients. They found the perfect place in the centre of Bognor Regis and, in an act of great faith, my mother and six of her Touch for Health colleagues clubbed together as partners to finance the first quarterly rent. The Touch for Health Centre was established and an Advisory Board and Committee elected to administer the Centre. The partners agreed to raise funds through offering membership and hold an Annual General Meeting and Sharing Day, to which all members and friends would be invited.

My mother wrote about the start up of the Centre in an article for The Balance Sheet.

"From this point on everything seemed to flow. Funds started to come in from supporters, furniture was either given or loaned, a couch and a wall clock were donated and many other items including stacking chairs from a church hall. Now TfH'ers (Touch for Health'ers) had a place of their own to meet for Balancing, holding workshops and meetings. There was one drawback - no running water - we had to go downstairs for it. Encouraged by the fact that income was sufficient for the next quarter, it was agreed to install the necessary facilities if something suitable could be found. A visit to a local scrap yard proved providential because a sink in pristine condition of the right size had been delivered recently. Needing a partner's approval, I found Maureen at home and together we set off to make the purchase. As it was a busy Saturday morning, we were concerned about parking near enough for unloading, but as we drove up outside the Centre, a car drove away leaving ample space to park. Maureen's husband happened to be available to help carry the sink upstairs and it was a perfect fit. Another member installed it and a plumber was called to connect to the water supply. The exact cost was met by an unexpected donation a few days later."

Help always seemed to come when it was needed and, in spite of their modest income, there was always enough money to pay the next quarter's rent. Once when it looked as if they were not going to make it, the very morning the payment was due, the Treasurer received a cheque for the exact amount! It seemed the Touch for Health Centre had come into being for a higher purpose and they were simply willing pawns in a bigger plan.

On 24 April 1988, a year after the promotion day, the Touch for Health Centre was officially opened by Brian Butler. It was the first of its kind in the country and rapidly became a place where more and more people could experience for themselves the value of a Touch for Health Balance. In addition to providing a base for practice and teaching, the Centre also held talks and workshops on other aspects of complementary and alternative therapies. The Centre continued to grow and the partners applied for charity status, which was granted in 1990, thanks in particular to Maureen's effort and enthusiasm. A donation was received from the Telethon Trust to support work done for children through Educational Kinesiology. Thanks to Maureen, the Kinesiology Federation was established to represent professional Kinesiologists. My mother became a professional member in 1992 and was recognised as a Registered Instructor of the Foundation Level Kinesiology Syllabus in 1995. She was later awarded a Fellowship in 2002.

A group of Touch for Health practitioners booked stands at exhibitions and natural health shows around the area to introduce the technique to a wider audience. Armed with couches and plenty of water, my mother and her colleagues set up their stand and waited. It was never long before they were working. If ever there was a lull in activity, they took to Balancing themselves to give one another an energy boost. However, this rarely happened because most of the time there was a continual cluster of people around their stand, like bees around a lavender bush.

In March 1995, John Thie arrived from America to teach at the Touch for Health Centre and my mother attended his two day Update Workshop. At the end of his visit, he sent a message saying how much he had enjoyed spending time with them all and thanking the Committee for helping to share his vision of what he hoped a Touch for Health Centre would achieve. John Thie returned to the United Kingdom in 1997 to share more of his knowledge and expertise and always appreciated the warm welcome he received from the Touch for Health practitioners at the Centre.

CHAPTER 14

AN INSPIRED HEALER

My mother's devotion to her healing work consumed her mind, body and soul. To understand as much as she could about the healing process, she attended numerous courses on related subjects, including: One Brain; Hyperton X; Optimum Health Balance; Health Kinesiology and Kinergetics, as well as The Radiance Technique (Real Reiki) and Esoteric Healing (Subtle Energy Healing). She tape-recorded every course she attended to go through it again and make further notes, in case she had missed something. Her healing ability expanded along with her knowledge and it was during the Esoteric Healing course she began to sense energy flowing through her brow chakra in the middle of her forehead. She described it by saying she simply needed to link into a person or situation and the energy started to flow, when enough energy had been taken, the flow stopped. She said it was not something she could turn on and off at will.

Her enhanced ability to sense energy led her to develop her own style of Guided Kinesiology and she created very detailed protocols to access the depth of the investigation. Her refined system of muscle testing needed only the slightest movement of the client's arm as a navigator to identify the location of the imbalances. It was like following a map searching for buried treasure in the ocean of the unconscious. With each new Balance she realised the key lay in connecting with the wisdom of the body, which has all the answers already and she was merely acting as a facilitator to connect with the inner healer within each one of her clients, as it is in all of us. As she learned more and more about the workings of the human body, she never ceased to be amazed at the interconnectedness of all parts. Her overwhelming desire and intention was to relieve the pain and stress for everyone who turned to her for help. She could not let someone off her couch unless they were in balance, which sometimes took between two or three hours. Many times, clients who had suffered from chronic pain for years and could hardly manage to climb the stairs to the treatment room, left with a new flexibility of movement and free of pain, with smiles on their faces.

Eventually, she decided to work from her home rather than at the Touch for Health Centre. She converted a bedroom in her house into a treatment room, setting up her couch and hanging diagrams on the wall of the Five Elements, the Chakra System, the Meridian Energy System and Human Anatomy. Her collection of tester kits, crystals, flower remedies and other equipment lay in drawers ready to hand, along with numerous scan sheets and protocols. Her library of books grew from deeply esoteric and spiritual to health, nutrition and different modalities of healing as she avidly read and absorbed information like a sponge. Her thirst for knowledge expanded along with her mind and her abilities as she increased her understanding of the workings of the human body. With every Balance she gave, her newfound knowledge was put into practice as she often read about a topic which related to her next client.

In addition to her client practice, my mother continued to teach Touch for Health and other related subjects. After attending the Hyperton Teacher's Workshop, she was able to put her knowledge to the test, on herself. She wrote of her experience in the next issue of The Balance Sheet.

"On my way back from London, my car was hit by another car as I turned into my son's home. I sustained a sideways whiplash and a nasty blow to the side

of my head, shoulder and right side. I held my ESR (emotional stress release) points as I staunched the blood, took Rescue Remedy and started using all the techniques we know to help balance ourselves. On the insistence of the Police, I had to be taken to Casualty and had the indignity of having my scalp 'stapled', rather fittingly referred to by my young granddaughter as having staple-isers! The following day was when Hyperton came into it's own. I called on a TfH colleague, who helped me with a more thorough Balance because I was very stiff, battered and bruised. What we noticed was the blow to the head was on Neurovascular Point 10 and this drew our attention to the number of muscles, which are affected by that point. Sure enough, all of those muscles relevant to NV10 on the right side were weak. We corrected the particular seven leg muscles and the Abdominals hypertonically, starting with the priority which was the Fascia Lata and to my amazement and delight, my neck and shoulder muscles were subsequently eased without further need of working on them. I have much to be thankful for."

Once again, it seemed that new knowledge had arrived at exactly the right moment.

As the Touch for Health practitioners developed their knowledge and experience, they found more ways to work with newly learned skills and techniques. One of these was to give a surrogate Balance for a client who was too ill or in too much pain to be balanced directly. In these cases, my mother worked with a Touch for Health colleague who 'locked-in' to the client's problems. The surrogate lay on the couch with the client sitting on a chair alongside, keeping contact by holding her arm. Working through the surrogate and doing the corrections on her, the necessary adjustments were transferred to the person being balanced. It sounds weird, but true. An extension of this technique developed when my mother realised when she was talking to someone on the telephone who needed help, she could tune-in to the person and do the adjustments on herself for the caller's benefit. I experienced this many times and felt the energy flowing into me simply from talking with her. Even if she wasn't available, picking up the phone with the intention of asking for help, made me feel better almost immediately.

Despite never advertising her healing work, clients came through recommendation and before long, my mother was seeing up to three clients a day and sometimes evenings and weekends. She devoted herself utterly to her healing. When she took a week off, *"to sort myself out"* as she put it, she never refused a call for help and as such her time-outs became increasingly few. As her reputation spread, new clients kept coming and the telephone hardly stopped ringing. She received calls and requests for help from people living overseas who had heard about her through friends. Distance did not seem to matter, she only needed a request or permission from the client to tune-in to the problem and energy began to flow through her brow chakra. The throbbing stopped when the client had received enough energy. It was as if the tap was magically turned off.

With a wealth of information stored in her mind, each client brought the opportunity to put into practice all her knowledge and skills. Always needing to understand the smallest detail of how something worked, she wrote copious annotations in the margins and underlined important points in many of her treasured books. Her insatiable desire to learn more led her to constantly have more to learn. It was a never-ending cycle and she began to understand that the greatest teacher is within each of us. All we have to do is access our inner guidance to take us there. She began to realise it was her inner guidance transforming her exactly as it was transforming her clients during the Balances she gave. The throbbing in her brow centre indicated which way to go and her acute sense of the change in a muscle navigated her down paths into previously unknown realms of the workings of the human body.

An expansion in her knowledge came through working with Charles Benham, who developed a technique called Optimum Health Balance. This method used icons or geometrical symbols to represent the vibration of different imbalances. By placing them on the body, the indicator muscle would weaken or strengthen. With the help of Kevin Pugh, a friend and TfH colleague, they devised a range of scan sheets of vibrational symbols with the blessing of Charles, to form the basis of Joan's own kinesiology modality, Guided Kinesiology. These scan sheets allowed access to the deepest level of imbalance in the person and it was this depth produced by Guided Kinesiology, which gave remarkable results. Identifying the origin of the trauma or imbalance at the deepest level enabled the blocked energy to be released, the cells revert to their natural state of balance and the wellbeing of the body restored.

On a personal level, I experienced many Balances and can truly say I would not be who I am today without my mother's guiding hand balancing me in my hours of need. She was there for all her family, not only helping us with our physical being, but also expanding our awareness and understanding about who we are and the wisdom of the body, which can be accessed through kinesiology. She was not only a mother and grandmother, but also a role model, mentor, teacher and guide to us and all her clients, who turned to her for help.

CHAPTER 15

SHARED MEMORIES AND TESTIMONIALS

My mother's Touch for Health colleagues shared their respect for her. She was seen as the mother figure, always caring and giving and supporting them as they supported her. She set high standards in her professional approach to her work and was always willing and eager to share her vast knowledge helping them to expand and develop their own potential. In addition to her private client work, a group of colleagues met at her house every Thursday evening for the purpose of sending healing to the greater good of all. A member of the group, Jacky McBroome, shared her memories of these evenings.

"The Thursday Group, or Felpham Group as I've also heard it called, met at Joan's house for 12 years or so from the early 1990s, weekly, for most of that time, less often towards the end. It began after some members of the Touch for Health Centre were guided to do a group Balance (energy work) coinciding with a major sun eclipse. We sent out healing for the planet and for various Earth energy centres like London and Tokyo, to allow energy to flow and harmonise for the areas of focus. The coincidences were amazing, down to what each of us turned up wearing related to the colours of the crystals and which we were guided to use within the work. We realised this kind of energy

work with group dynamics was too important to leave there, which was why some of us decided to meet regularly and Joan offered the use of her house.

"*It settled down with usually a core group of four or five people with some joining and some leaving after a while. It was a support and friendship group as well with sometimes a lot of chat. I came to realise it didn't matter if we spent time catching up with one another because often deep understandings fell out of those conversations too. We were all so connected. Often, the issue that had been going on during the week for one of the members also figured largely for the others. A small example was one time where the discussion was about being joyful and one of us had been to a dinner party where he was sitting next to not one, but between two ladies called Joy!*

"*We usually began our work with a meditation to attune to the heart space of each other and with the Guides who were there supporting and working through us, so that subsequent work was coming from a harmonious and focused energetic space. A lot of our energy work was distant healing, for people, for situations, for places. We brought in knowledge from kinesiology, dowsing, crystals, colour, from inner guidance and intuition and more. Joan was amazing in her extensive reading around medical subjects and she produced scan charts she used for evaluation and healing of her clients, in tiny writing, with so much information on each sheet of paper. I once tried to make one of these sheets neater for her, so other people could read it, but it defeated me because I couldn't get it all onto one computer page.*

"*One project, which was particularly important, was the Rose Quartz Mother Crystal. We were guided to acquire a fabulous pyramid-shaped rose quartz and it was programmed through us in meditation by Spirit. I can't capture the extent of the energy programme, but shall we say it was based around harmony for the planet. We subsequently sourced tiny crystals, sometimes crystal dust and this was placed next to the Mother Crystal to absorb its programme. These baby crystals were distributed far and wide via friends and contacts right across the world. Of course, we will never know the effect of this work and it's not for us to know. But it was offered up by the Thursday group with love and with intent for the highest good of all life.*

"For me the Thursday Group was like a heartbeat going through those years, it was so important. We laughed, we chatted, we learned, we directed energy, with light and fun and clear intent for harmony and healing."

Other Touch for Health colleagues have also kindly shared their memories of my mother and their experiences of working with her.

'When Touch For Health was introduced to England from America, a group of like-minded people learnt this new system of muscle testing and needed somewhere to practice their new skills. The TfH Centre was opened in Bognor Regis and it was here I first met Joan Brownrigg. I was a little in awe of this elegant lady who in her quiet way helped in the setting up of the Centre. Joan was never flustered, never had a hair out of place, she had a vast knowledge of the human body and always knew which book had relevant information. What's more, she usually had that book in her bag. As I got to know Joan, I was very aware of her gentle approach to her clients, her caring and skill in balancing their energies to promote the optimum health for each of them.

"Joan's aim to achieve Optimum Health for all her clients came from working closely with Charles Benham who created the Optimum Health Balance. Joan attended many of Charles's workshops because always, she wanted more knowledge. Having acquired the knowledge she generously shared learning with any of us wanting to learn more. We had some really interesting balancing from both Joan and Charles. Two or three times a year, a car load of us drove to High Wycombe, where Charles lived and he gave us all an individual Balance, Joan called them our MOTs for the year. Afterwards, we went out to lunch at his favourite eating hostel, a very important part of the day.

"Representing the Centre, we attended many Health Exhibitions, again Joan insisted on very high standards. We all wore navy trousers with white tee shirts and sweatshirts with the TfH logo printed on both. On these occasions, we learnt so much from being with Joan. She felt like a mother figure to us all and gave us the confidence to Balance alongside of her. If anyone forgot a sweatshirt, Joan always had a spare one in her bag. She gave me the confidence to give an impromptu half-hour talk on TfH at these venues, which I never would have thought possible. I even got to enjoy these sessions.

'*Because Joan was so professional and caring with her clients, she saw many people who were either in great pain, or very unwell and had very little energy, sometimes they couldn't respond to the muscle testing. At the Centre we all knew it was possible to work through a third person called a surrogate. Through practice at the Centre, it was decided that my body was suitable to be a surrogate body. The client sat comfortably by the couch, I lay on the couch, fully clothed, the client contacted my arm and Joan, who was balancing, worked using my muscles to give her the information she needed to balance the client. When linked up I felt the pain of the client and often some of the emotions involved, I never needed to know any details. As Joan collected the information she needed, which was always very thorough and could take an hour or more, the client sometimes closed their eyes. At the right time, Joan balanced the client and usually their pain or problem was helped. Always there was benefit, they looked happier and felt less stressed. Sometimes it took a day and they telephoned to say how much better they were and thanking Joan. She really was a remarkable lady. When the Balance was finished, Joan always was caring for her surrogate, making sure none of the client's problems stayed with me. More than that, my body had received a balance, my muscles all tuned and I felt charged with energy.*

"*Whenever we all met at the Centre and Joan was with us, we knew we would learn more ways to help our clients. She left us so much information and love. It has been an enormous privilege to have known Joan and worked beside her. I often feel her energy is still around us. I may be thinking how shall I tackle this or that and I wonder how would Joan tackle this? Well, she would want to get to the reason for the problem and work her way through it. With love, Sheila Hawkes.*"

Another colleague and friend, Binky Slade, had her own experience of a Joan Balance when she had been diagnosed with a cancerous lump in her breast and was advised to have surgery, followed by chemotherapy and possible radiotherapy.

"*I wanted my body to have the best chance of healing itself and to do all I could to promote that before my operation. How blessed I was to receive so much healing love and prayers from my fabulous family and friends. I went to Joan's house for what I thought would be about an hour's Touch for Health Balance. I should have known better! Joan with her good friend and dedicated assistant, Sheila, there to help throughout, worked on me for about four and a half hours! Not only did Joan use the TfH system for energy balancing helping me with a whole body Balance awareness and insightful new perspectives, she also dug deep working at the highest level, I felt on all energy levels, mind, body and spirit. Her approach may have been influenced by her association and work with her close friend and mentor, Charles Benham who originated the Optimum Health Balance system of Kinesiology in the 1990s. Joan, like Charles, got into those higher dimensions, subtle and vibrational, which can heal on the cellular level. Joan used all the tools in her toolbox, as Sheila said and I went through a gamut of emotions from crying to laughter, immense shaking to deep calm, a catharsis like no other. After my session with Joan, I went to see Charles who muscle tested me with one of his vibrational icons (visual symbols). I had the operation and the prognosis afterwards was there were no cancerous cells in the lump or surrounding tissue and no further treatment was necessary.*

"There are several ways a person can achieve complete healing: to come into contact with healing energy, whatever that may be; to have a therapist or healer who acts as a channel for healing energy; or to use something that contains healing energy. I feel Joan did all those things for me, except Joan always said after any TfH or healing session, "Well done, you have done it yourself!"

"All I know is I felt Joan's Balance got to the depths of me, peeling beneath the hidden layers and helped me to release whatever negative emotions resided in me, which may have been the trigger for the cancerous cells. I am so very grateful to have known and experienced prodigious and generous Joan, as a friend, teacher and healer in my life and feel exceedingly blessed to have benefited from her healing love, from my heart."

In addition to her colleagues, my mother was also held in high regard by other therapists and professionals. Nick Poole, a Chartered Psychologist shares his thoughts.

"Joan Brownrigg was an inspiration to me. She accepted her clients with all of their frailties and was prepared to work with their concerns to achieve the best possible outcome for them at whatever stage of transformation they were. She was non-judgemental and forgiving and I found enormous comfort and inspiration in her intelligent and loving presence. In days of increasingly intrusive regulation, Joan helped me as a psychologist, to feel entirely comfortable to confidently explore the more esoteric aspects of human individuality and question the pre-eminent relevance and status of "evidence-based" research, especially when fraudulently employed to indiscriminately support pathological thinking on an international scale. I was intrigued by Joan's approach. Once I had accepted the authenticity and integrity of her wisdom and intention, I was comfortable to not know exactly what was happening because of the potency of the feeling of healing she was able to engender in me, so that I could get out of the way of my own healing.

"What's the lesson for me? To aspire to create the same atmosphere of welcoming acceptance and respect for the people I encounter. Thank you Joan. Nick."

Joan on a TFH training day

CHAPTER 16

IN SERVICE

My mother's devotion to her healing work gave her little time for anything else, although she did her best to keep some days free to catch up with jobs around the house and garden, which she always kept tidy and filled with flowers. Even so she always made herself available to the family and we usually called on her to babysit or keep an eye on our houses and our menagerie of animals when we were on holiday. She insisted on returning home despite invitations to stay and as much as she was willing to help us, I am sure she breathed a sigh of relief when we returned. Holidays in Spain were no longer on her agenda since Viola had moved back to England after Frank died and was now living in a small apartment in Bognor Regis. It was lovely for them to live near to one another and their bond remained very close. I made a regular afternoon visit when my daughter started singing lessons in Felpham after school. Our tea-time slot became sacrosanct and a permanent date in the diary for many years.

During her Touch for Health training and sharing days, my mother kept herself in Balance with the help of her colleagues. However, when she stopped teaching to focus solely on her client work, the opportunities were not so readily available. As more and more people came for Balances, she took less time for herself. Often the phone started ringing before breakfast and she was still on the phone when the first client arrived whose Balance could go on until early afternoon, by which time the next client was ringing the doorbell. Sometimes she had no time to eat more than a quick snack between appointments and often said jokingly, *"I've just had my breakfast!"* when it was late afternoon. When she did get herself a meal, either the telephone rang or someone came to the door. With her advancing age, we were concerned about her wellbeing and suggested she take the telephone off the hook while she had something to eat, as she did when she was working. Our suggestion was only met with, *"What happens if one of you need me?"* Despite assurances we could wait, it made no difference to her willingness to be constantly available for anyone who required healing. Her eating habits became more erratic and it took many a persuasive plea before she joined the family for a proper meal, something she had always enjoyed regularly before. Despite this, however, her energy levels remained remarkably high. She maintained she received as much energy as she gave out during the Balances. Unless her body gave her an enforced time-out with a migraine, her health remained good.

Even so she was not immune from needing medical intervention herself which happened when she had a choking episode while trying to eat quickly before a client arrived. Some years previously she had a parotid gland removed, which made chewing difficult and each mouthful needed to be taken slowly. However, in the rush to eat, her oesophagus went into spasm and she was unable to swallow. She rang her doctor who immediately referred her to the local Accident and Emergency Unit. My mother's response was she couldn't possibly go because she had a diary filled with client appointments. As her throat had calmed down, she did not go to the hospital until a couple of days later. The doctor wanted to see what might have caused the spasm, which necessitated inserting a tube down her oesophagus. The tube would not go down easily and some force was used resulting in considerable stress and trauma to her throat. No abnormalities were found and the doctor prescribed medication to calm the throat. However, after her stressful experience, she was reluctant to swallow a pill and had the notion of energising a crystal with the vibration of the medication, placing the crystal in a glass of water and drinking the water.

Within a few days her throat recovered, but the trauma of the experience left its mark as she was left with permanent discomfort in her diaphragm and fear it might happen again. The lasting effects resulted in her reluctance to eat solid food and from then on she limited her diet to liquids or soft food, with vitamins and supplements to support her diet. Her energy levels remained good nonetheless and she was able to do the gardening, tidy the house and catch up with the piles of books, journals and articles she had to read. With so much reading to do, she signed up for a course on speed-reading over two weekends. The assignment in between was to read five books on a subject of choice. While any subject would be taxing, my mother chose to read about the brain, perhaps the most complex organ in the human body. She returned to the workshop for the second weekend with the contents of all five books lodged in her memory bank, hopefully only a thought away. Whether or not she ever needed to access the information was never disclosed but it was another indicator of her willingness to go the extra mile to achieve a result.

CHAPTER 17

RETIREMENT

During the 20 years my mother was involved with Touch for Health she built up a busy practice with clients coming to see her from all parts of the country and indeed, from across the world as her reputation spread far and wide. Her serene and loving presence, together with her considerable knowledge and wisdom, created a safe space for other people to unburden their troubled hearts and minds and help their body to regain balance. She was held in high regard for the integrity of her approach to her work, she remained humble in her achievements and the first to acknowledge she was merely a facilitator in her healing ability. The knowledge she gained from the many years of Balances she facilitated for her clients expanded her understanding of the miraculous way the human body works and how disease manifests from imbalances in the subtle energy fields.

In 2005, my mother's expertise and the admiration she received from her colleagues was recognised at the International Kinesiology Conference in Keele, Staffordshire, when she received the Kinesiology United Kingdom Award in recognition of her contribution to the growth and development of Kinesiology. Her nomination came as a great surprise to her and the award was presented to her at the Touch for Health Annual General Meeting and Sharing Day. At the age of 86, when most people had been retired for at least 20 years, she was completely immersed in her work and committed to being in service. Her greatest desire was to continue to assist those people who needed her and she never refused a request for help. As far as we knew, she had never given any thought or intention of retiring and giving up her healing practice.

Sometimes, however, the desires of the little self have to bow to the needs of the greater Self. This begins as a subtle whisper in the ear or a nudge on the shoulder to indicate that maybe it is time to slow down and take life a little easier. These subtle hints began to appear through her erratic eating patterns and occasionally getting inaccurate information in her Balances, which disturbed her because she always followed detailed protocols to get the information she needed before beginning the treatment. She was feeling tired more often with occasional breathlessness, as well as becoming forgetful and repeating the same things. None of which were particularly unusual in someone of her age.

However, one afternoon in late November 2006, an unexpected event changed the course of her life forever. She was driving out of a supermarket car park and another car come up on the inside lane and their cars collided. Fortunately, no one was hurt, but mum was naturally shocked and upset. The side of her car was damaged but she was able to drive home. She arranged for an insurance agent to come to her house to assess the damage to the car a few days later. They were looking at the car when she suddenly felt dizzy and breathless and told the agent she needed to sit down and continue their conversation indoors. I telephoned her to find out what the insurance agent had said but she sounded so strange I sensed something was wrong and immediately drove round to see her. When I arrived, she appeared confused, emotional and unlike her normal self. It was possible that talking about the accident and looking at the car brought the trauma to the surface and delayed shock literally took her breath away.

The incident had a far deeper effect on her than anyone realised at the time. With her resources running on low, her body did not have a reserve energy tank to call on. David and I decided to keep a closer eye on her and either called or visited every day. She had no option but to cancel all appointments she had in her diary. Almost immediately the telephone stopped ringing. After months and months of continual telephone calls from new and existing clients asking for appointments, suddenly no one rang. It was as if the Universe had decreed, time-out. The subtle whispers had been ignored and the greater Self had spoken loud and clear. The message was obvious and she was forced to listen.

Mum expected to resume her client work after a few days rest but as the days and weeks passed, she didn't feel strong enough to see anyone and had to accept for the time being her healing days were on hold. After all those years of saying, *"I wish I had time to sort my stuff out,"* finally the time had come, although not in the way she wanted or planned. Her enforced retirement now gave her the time and opportunity to go through all the papers, books, files and articles she had accumulated during the years. These were not tasks that could be undertaken easily, especially with a confused mind, yet, it was as if they all had to be done at once and her sitting room became covered in papers. Almost overnight, her orderly house with nothing out of place became an untidy, disorganised place of chaos.

She began giving away her possessions as though preparing to go on a journey and wanting to pass onto other people what she no longer needed. Always a squirrel at heart and keeping things just in case they might be of future use, every room was a storehouse, from the garage, to the loft, to her den and her treatment room. She spent every day sitting in her chair surrounded by books, papers, pens, pencils, going through everything, reluctant to throw much away. This was not the mother we were used to seeing. The walls of perfection had cracked.

CHAPTER 18

TIME TO HEAL

Slowly, mum recovered albeit with a nasty cough, which disturbed her at night as soon as she lay down. She also had a wound on her leg which was taking time to heal. A few weeks before, she had tried to rescue a little bird trapped in the garage and was pulling boxes aside to find the bird, when a pole fell and struck her leg. She hardly noticed the impact at the time being so intent on rescuing the bird, but she later discovered a nasty gash on her calf. She cleaned the wound, but it remained open and sore. It reminded her of the ulcers and wounds she had seen on her grandmother's leg when she was a child. Gradually, the wound healed but it was an indication of her poor circulation.

Mum had every intention of returning to work and driving her newly restored car and couldn't wait to get back to her old self. She found having time on her hands without working difficult to cope with. All her life she had lived to a purpose. Now it seemed as though everything had been taken away from her and she was left with nothing but herself. She was in complete resistance to her new state of being and found it difficult to accept she could no longer function in the same way. Her mind and heart were willing to be in service, but her body was reluctant to respond.

After a few weeks, her energy gradually began to return and clients occasionally rang asking for her help. She was delighted to find she could still sense energy when tuning-in and be of help, albeit in a different way. She was able to walk around slowly and enjoyed getting out in the fresh air and going for a drive in the car. By the spring, she felt she had some sort of her life back, even if it was very different from what she had known before. However, her mind remained confused and she found it difficult to remember what had recently happened and eventually had to accept she could no longer drive. As an independent person, she felt the loss of her car acutely. She had always disliked being beholden to other people and relying on anyone else and had developed a fierce sense of independence. She had been able to rely on her own resources all her life, but these were now limited. Her meagre diet during the years had taken its toll and she lost interest in food. We arranged for carers to visit and make sure she had something to eat, which she resisted at first, reluctant to admit she needed support from anyone outside the family. However, eventually she accepted their help realising her family could not be with her all the time.

While her short-term memory was poor, she began to recall experiences from her childhood, her school life, the war and everything that had happened before leaving Argentina for good. Memories which had lain deeply buried began to surface from the depths of her unconscious. She had experienced so much in her life, both good times and bad, but it was the bad she was now focusing on. All she talked about was the pain, loss and suffering she had been through during her life. With the memories came the emotions as the anger and hatred surfaced about the way she felt being teased by her cousins when she was little and her parents sending her to school in England. She even said she hated being born in London and wished she could have been born in her beloved Argentina like her sisters.

It was as though she had pressed the replay button of her life's story and was watching the events and situations replaying themselves in her mind like a movie. She relived each moment as if it had just happened and the buried emotions at last had a voice. The look of fear in her eyes as she described her war-time experiences; her feelings of helplessness and shock when she witnessed the plane crash on the airbase and bombs landing leaving nothing but death and destruction, dust and debris before her eyes and despair as she held a dying man in her arms. The trauma she had been through and carried inside of her for so long was being brought to the light for all to witness. This was a side of her no one had seen before. She had never shown much emotion, keeping everything very close to her heart and on the surface everything was always 'fine.' We learned more about her life in those few months than we had ever known before. Along with the memories, came the emotions, guilt, frustration, anger, sorrow and sadness, which had been locked away for so many years. It was as though she was witnessing a life that wasn't her own.

For someone who spent her life healing other people, now she was finally healing herself. With all the knowledge and skills at her fingertips, it would have been easy for her to let go of the emotional trauma undisturbed for so many years, except she seemed unable to remember what she had done to help other people. It was as if the connection to her inner guidance was cut off leaving her helpless and alone. Knowing how she had helped so many people and yet seemed unable or unwilling to help herself was a challenge for us all to witness. We could only stand back and be there for her trusting whatever was happening was in Divine Order and she was being supported in ways we could not understand.

Sometimes unexpected things happen that turn out unexpectedly for the best as happened the day I took mum to the dentist to have a crown replaced. I was sitting in the waiting room while she was being seen when I was called into the treatment room. Mum was lying in the chair and the dentist explained the crown had slipped out of her fingers and it had disappeared down mum's throat. Mum was having difficulty swallowing and she had telephoned the hospital for advice and said mum needed to be taken to hospital for an x-ray. Mum appeared calm despite the obvious stress of the situation.

We drove to the local hospital for the x-ray which showed the crown nestled low down in her throat and were advised to go to the nearest Ear Nose and Throat unit for further investigation, which was 20 miles away. Mum was told 'nil by mouth' in case she needed an anaesthetic. At least four hours had passed since her breakfast and I was worried about her fragile state without any nourishment as well as the added stress of a crown stuck in her throat. We arrived at the hospital and waited three hours before the doctor could see her. On investigation, the offending object had disappeared under a bubble of fluid and could not be seen. The doctor advised admitting mum for further investigation under anaesthetic. Miraculously, a vacant bed was found and within a short time mum was sitting on the bed connected to a glucose drip as they could tell she was dehydrated. The doctor hoped she would be going to the theatre as soon as possible. It was now eight hours since we had left home, the day had not turned out as planned and the next two had not been scheduled in the diary as 'recovery from trauma of swallowing a crown.' However, when things happen out of the blue, all we can do is surrender and accept life has other plans and go with the flow. Despite the trauma, mum seemed perfectly happy and completely at ease, enjoying the attention she was receiving and watching the activities of the ward with interest. The drip was having its effect and she was positively blossoming. On the other hand I had the prospect of another 40 mile round trip to collect an overnight case for her which did not fill me with joy during evening rush hour. When I returned, mum was sitting up in bed looking very relaxed, insisting that because she was now beginning to swallow she wanted to go home. However, the procedure had not yet taken place and the doctor was reluctant to let her go without an investigation because there was a risk of the crown becoming dislodged and ending up somewhere that could be life-threatening. Mum had no option, but to settle down for the night and I left her knowing she was in the best possible place.

Early next morning, I telephoned the ward for an update and was told the procedure had been carried out but the crown had not been found and it was assumed it was making its own way out of her body. I arrived on the ward to find mum looking very regal and certainly in a better state than she had been when I left her, thanks to the care and attention she was receiving. As much as she wanted to go home, the doctor felt it best for her to stay in another night for observation. She was discharged home the following day. Apart from the initial delays, we were both impressed with the care and attention she received and mum seemed to enjoy her unexpected hospital experience. She was grateful to everyone who looked after her and her only complaint was that the doctors no longer wore white coats.

It was fortunate the incident did not have any lasting effects like her previous hospital experience. Instead it took away her fears of doctors and hospitals and she now saw them in a new light. For someone who had shunned the medical profession for herself, she had always suggested a visit to the doctor if it was appropriate. Her healing work focused on a deeper and energetic level unravelling the messages the body gives in pain or discomfort, but not everyone is able to understand these subtle messages because they require a degree of self-awareness, which develops through time. It seemed contrary to her own practice to suggest a visit to the doctor. However, she had the wisdom to know that an integrated approach to healthcare was the most beneficial.

With her increasing frailty, carers and family members visited her regularly during the day. I made soup for her from our abundant vegetable garden, which kept her nourished as much as possible along with the nutritional drinks prescribed by her doctor. Somehow she managed to keep going even though her body showed signs of weakening. We moved her chair to the window as she loved watching the birds in her garden. This simple act brought her much joy and she insisted we feed them every morning. She had her favourites and loved the little birds and got cross when the larger ones flew down and drove the smaller ones away. She shooed them away waving her arm at the window, they disappeared for a moment, but soon flew back not leaving until the final breadcrumb was pecked. A pair of seagulls roosted each year on the roof of her house raising their young. She loved seeing the tiny little fledglings like bundles of fluff sitting on the roof. Their parents were very protective and flew at any intruder, yet whenever any of us approached the house, they left us alone, perhaps aware they were welcome tenants. They returned each year, having found a desirable rooftop residence and seemed reluctant to look elsewhere.

CHAPTER 19

LETTING GO

Despite the challenges mum was going through, her coping mechanism throughout her life had made her strong enough to deal with everything life gave her. Now as she neared the end of her life, she was facing perhaps the greatest challenge of all. She had always been a tower of strength for us and we looked to her for support and it seemed she would go on forever. She was a true inspiration and a mentor to us all, a beacon of light who helped pull us out of our darkness when we were lost. We turned to her for guidance and she willingly supported us until we were strong enough on our own again. But virtually overnight she had changed from being the dynamic, determined, independent woman we had known to a frail, elderly lady needing care and support. As much as she loved her work, her total commitment to helping other people had sacrificed her own needs, which were now crying out for attention. Her sudden and enforced retirement had unexpectedly given her the space she unconsciously needed to heal herself.

Now it was our turn to be there for her, holding her hands, supporting her in her hour of need because she had to find her inner strength and learn to accept help from other people. I sensed the battle going on within her as she resisted her state of being, wanting to return to her previous state of health, yet her mind and body were unwilling to co-operate. We could do nothing to take away her suffering, except listen and support her through her darkest hours, as she had held us lovingly in her hands whenever we had needed her.

She drifted into a troubled world where the present was increasingly less real to her as her spirit was gently guiding her to let go little by little. Perhaps she knew on her soul level that it was all perfectly planned and we were merely observers of a higher plan. As much as she wanted to stay, she was longing for peace and freedom of her spirit, unencumbered by its physical form and as much as we longed for her suffering to end, letting her go was difficult for us as well. With the many losses and separations she experienced during her lifetime, I sensed it was this final separation from her loved ones, which was making it hard to let go.

She kept repeating, *"Lord, please help me. Lord, please help me,"* calling on her faith, which had been with her all her life. She knew well enough she needed to let go of her physical form for her spirit to reach its heavenly home. Home is a word, which creates images, memories and emotions that have a powerful effect on every level of our being. We call our house our home and yet we also say home is where the heart is because it is where we feel at home that matters most. For mum it had always been Argentina, the land she called home and loved with a passion, which remained forever in her heart. Leaving Argentina had broken her heart and she vowed she would never go back. When I asked her why, she answered, *"Because I could not bear leaving again."* This I could understand yet, unlike her, I longed to go back and when I finally did, I knew what she meant. Each time I left, my heart cried from leaving a place I love with every cell of my being. It is like a grief that goes so deep, beyond the reach of words to describe.

I am not sure mum ever really settled in England and consequently distracted herself as much as she could to bury the pain. Whenever she spoke about her life in Argentina, her eyes sparkled and you sensed the joy in her heart and the passion in her voice. As she recalled those years, the memories surfaced and the emotions were strong. Perhaps she knew she was not meant to return and buried her heartache deep within herself because the loss and grief of separation were too much to bear.

The weeks and months passed and one afternoon, as she was looking out of the window watching the birds, I heard her say clearly, *"There is nothing left for me now, I might as well go."* I felt a chill move across my heart. I knew she had finally surrendered and was ready to move on. Until that moment, she had been unwilling to let go. As she spoke those words, she unconsciously flicked the switch that was to take her spirit home. Her condition deteriorated and within a week she was admitted to hospital with pneumonia, a condition often referred to as 'old man's friend' because it helps to take someone gently to the other side. It had come for my father 34 years before, I could sense he was with her now, watching and waiting for her to make her final crossing.

She slipped away early one morning before David and I could be with her. I walked over to her beside and saw her lying so peacefully, I thought she was sleeping, until David said, *"She has gone."* I kissed her forehead and said goodbye, silently screaming through my tears, *Mum, you could have waited for us. Why did you leave without saying goodbye?* I had expected to be with her, wanting to be there holding her hand and hearing her final out breath. And yet in my heart I knew it was what she wanted. She had left knowing we were on our way before we were able to reach her.

Our beloved mother had let go of her physical body and returned to spirit. She could now rest in peace. I was happy for her that her suffering had ended but I felt a hole opening in my heart that once held her close. She had been the heart of our family. We had our memories and the love we had shared and would have to get used to living without her and that wouldn't be easy.

I went to see her in the Chapel of Rest. She looked serene and at peace with almost a smile on her face. I placed a freshly cut rose from the garden in her hands and said a final farewell. I knew she was no longer there but even so found it hard to say goodbye to her physical form. I felt her presence in the room and knew she had been watching me for she sent me a message, *"Tell Jeanine, I am not the body."*

We arranged her funeral with family and friends joining together in love and gratitude to honour an amazing woman who had been an inspiration to all those whose lives she had touched. Her pioneering spirit and deep love for her family and friends extended to all humanity and Mother Earth. She had willingly offered herself in selfless service in her quiet, gentle way, with a serene presence, power and wisdom and healing hands, forever humble knowing she was simply an instrument, willing to be of service to her fellow travellers on their earthly journey. Her memory lives on in us all.

PART 3

ME

THE WHITE HORSE

A mystical lake lies in the landscape created since time began. Beside the lake is a grove of ancient trees with the ability to connect whoever sits under them with insights into their imagination.

I came upon this lake by chance one day when out for a walk. My footsteps guided me to sit for while and enjoy the beauty of the lake. The day was hot and cloudless. It felt good to be out of the sun and rest. I sat down on the grass in the shade and relaxed against a tree, its branches enfolding me like angel wings.

I must have fallen asleep because suddenly I was awakened by a loud noise, horse's hooves galloping across the ground. I looked round but saw no one, I listened again and all was silent. Strange, I thought, I wonder what that was? I lay back against the tree and my eyes gently closed again.

When I awoke, the sun was setting low on the horizon. I stood up and walked away from the lake, back down the pathway that had led me there. I arrived home and feeling tired, went to bed and fell into a deep sleep.

I woke suddenly. The same sound of horse's hooves galloping across the ground roused me from a deep sleep. I got out of bed and went to the window, drawing back the curtains to see if there was anyone riding at this time of night. Nothing, the night was silent, all was calm. I turned back to bed and lay down. Awake, I tried to work out what the noise was. Had I imagined it, and why twice in one day, when I had never heard anything like it before? It didn't make sense. Horses galloping indicated the rider was in a hurry, or perhaps the horse was rider-less, I hadn't seen anything so I had no way of knowing if there was a rider on the horse galloping its heart out. Whatever or whoever, the horse was in a hurry, a sense of urgency in its hooves as they clattered through my mind.

I fell back to sleep and woke with the sun streaming through my window. Another lovely summer's day. I jumped out of bed, and climbed into the shower and the water cleansed my body and soul. My thoughts drifted back to the sound I had heard in the night, but didn't dwell on it as I dressed in a hurry, a busy day lay ahead for me.

I was the editor of a fashion magazine and had a deadline for the printers today. All copy had to be agreed by midday and there was work to be done. I walked into the office and greeted my friend, Abby, who had worked with me for years and we had become good friends. I wondered about telling her about the horses, but didn't get a chance because work took over and the next few hours I had no time to think of anything else. We made the deadline and I suggested to Abby we have lunch together. We took our sandwiches and wandered into the nearby park. I noticed a tree similar to the one I had sat under by the lake which I had not noticed before, but perhaps I had never really looked at the trees. We sat down and started to eat our lunch. I began telling Abby about the weird sounds I had heard, wondering what she must think of me. But instead of laughing and dismissing it as a figment of my imagination, she told me a story she had once heard.

"Long ago, when time meant nothing at all, there lived a king in a land rich with milk and honey. The king had a beautiful daughter and he prized his daughter above all else in his kingdom. His wife, the queen, died giving birth to their daughter and he grieved his loss every time he looked at his child. She brought him pain and joy. The king knew his daughter was restless and longed for an adventure, for she was a child of free spirit and loved nothing more than to spend time in the gardens, talking to the trees and flowers. The king watched his daughter as she played and danced, so happily, as he sat with

tears in his heart seeing her live as his beloved wife lay buried in a cold dark grave. Life is so unjust, he thought, why was I given such a gift at the same time to lose what I loved most? Why couldn't I have both my wife and my daughter here beside me now?

His daughter longed for freedom, as much as she loved her father she hated being kept in the palace grounds and had no idea what lay beyond the stone walls. Often she asked her father to allow her out, but he always answered, "Why would you want to go outside, you have everything you need here. Tell me what it is you desire and I will order it to be brought to you."

The daughter smiled and thanked her father for his love and his generosity and asked for a white horse that she may ride on its back through the palace grounds.

The king immediately ordered the most beautiful white horse to be found and brought to him and when it appeared, he took his daughter to see his gift to her. His daughter thanked her father and gave him a kiss. She jumped on the horse's back and rode off through the palace grounds, disappearing so fast her father had no time to call the guards to prevent her from leaving.

Her father never saw his daughter again. The sound of the galloping horse haunted him for the rest of his life and he died grieving the loss of his beloved wife and daughter."

I looked at Abby as she finished telling the story. I had tears in my eyes. I felt deeply for the sadness of the king and at the same time, I felt the joy of his daughter as she galloped to her freedom. I didn't know what to say, I stood up and walked back to the office, leaving Abby following on behind.

Several weeks went by and I had no time to think about the horses or the tale Abby had told me. I had no more wakeful nights of horse's hooves galloping through my dreams. I forgot about it, as life took its relentless charge of keeping busy, going out, seeing friends, deadlines, catching up with the family, work, and more work. I was tired of the incessant wheel of existence and longed for a change. I needed time-out and I took myself off for the afternoon and walked back to the lake and sat once again beneath the ancient trees.

I fell asleep almost immediately but was then awakened by the sound of galloping hooves. This time I saw a vision of a young girl, her long hair blowing in the wind and the expression of joy etched across her face as she rode her beautiful white horse across the fields. She pulled up in front of me, the horse panting as he came to rest under the tree. She leant across and patted his neck and looked at me.

"Hello," she said, "I've seen you here before. Why do you come to this lake?"

I thought I was dreaming and answered her, "I love this lake, it helps me to feel calm, I live in a world where nothing ever stops and sometimes I need to escape."

"I know what you mean," she said, "my world felt like that, but I had to escape, it was destroying me."

Somehow I knew she was the girl in Abby's story.

"Did you leave your father to find peace?"

"Yes, I had to," she answered, "he did not understand. He kept me like a bird in a cage, I had to fly free."

"But he died of a broken heart," I said. "How can you live knowing that he suffered so much when you left?"

"I did not ask him to break his heart," she answered "that was the way he felt. If I had stayed, I would have died of a broken heart. I took the decision to live and not die and my spirit rides free now as he lies buried beneath the earth."

"Why have you come to see me?" I asked her.

"Because I am in you," she said, "your spirit longs to be free from the life you are living."

"Yes, that is true, that is why I come to this lake. Somehow it helps me to feel free."

"You can be free in your spirit and leave the prison world, if you want."

"How can I do that? I can't simply walk out of my job and my life."

"Well, I rode out of my life and look at me now. I have moved on and left everyone else behind."

"Yes, but you did not have a mortgage and bills to pay, a job and an office to run."

"No, but it doesn't matter what you do, you can always find freedom. Even if you stay, you simply have to look at life differently."

"How can I do that? It doesn't make sense. I feel trapped all the time, how can I find freedom when I can't move?"

"It's all in your mind," she answered. "Your mind is keeping you in prison, it is not your job, or your bills or mortgage, they are merely reasons your mind gives you to control you. The last thing the mind wants is you to be free."

"Why?' I asked.

"Because the mind likes to think it is in control and loves telling you what to do, where to go and why you have to work. Even if you don't like it, the more you complain, the more your mind will keep you where you are. It says it is keeping you safe when all the time it is scared of doing anything else and even more scared that you will stop listening to it."

"What happens if I stop listening to it? I didn't know I had a choice to listen to it or not?"

"Of course, you always have a choice, you can listen to your heart instead."

"Why my heart, what does that have to do with my mind?"

"Nothing, in fact, the last thing your mind wants you to do, is listen to your heart."

"Why is that?"

'Because you might simply do what you want and what makes you feel good and happy and all those wonderful feelings that mean you are living as a free spirit, like me. Your higher mind resides in your heart, it is your inner guidance."

"Did you listen to the inner guidance in your heart when you decided to jump on your horse and ride away from your father?"

"Yes, that is exactly what I did."

"But leaving him caused him so much heartbreak."

"I know, but that was because his mind wanted him to listen to all the reasons why he felt sad, that he had lost me forever and the more sad he felt, the *sadder he became until he could bear it no more and he died. If he had listened to his heart, he would have heard it saying, love your daughter enough to set her free, be happy that she is able to feel her spirit and ride away to happiness. If he had listened to his heart and not his mind, I would still be living in the palace because I could have come and gone and not be kept locked away."*

"Do I need to listen to my heart to set me free?"

"Yes, that is the only way to find freedom, follow your heart and begin your own adventure. Listen to your heart and you never know, you might find yourself riding a beautiful white horse like mine one day."

I smiled as she rode away on her beautiful horse. For deep in my heart was a longing to ride again across the pampas of my beloved homeland, feeling the freedom of my spirit in a land I loved. How had she known what lay in the deepest part of my being, the memories of a child doing what she loved most of all?

I walked back to my world with a glow in my heart that was not there before. I knew what I had to do, I would find that child again and set her free.

CHAPTER 20

RETURN TO ARGENTINA

The purpose of life is to live with love and joy in our hearts. It is easy to feel joyful when life is going well but not so easy when life is challenging and we face a crisis. We may feel out of control but we have to remember that no matter what life throws at us, we have a choice how to respond. To see challenges as opportunities to change and heal ourselves is like diving beneath the waves to search for treasure lying buried on the ocean floor. The treasure is the gift we can find if we have the courage to look at our shadows of the past where we can access our deep emotional wounds. Our tendency is to bury the past but any repressed emotions will continue to play out in our everyday reality until we are ready to let them go.

My mother never wanted to go back to Argentina and yet it is all I ever wanted to do. We both felt heartbroken leaving and we buried our pain. My mother created a busy life so she had no time to look within, I had the rest of my life to come. As I grew up, the sadness lessened, but the deep yearning in my heart to return never left. When the first opportunity arrived, thanks to a generous 21st birthday gift from my aunt and uncle, unexpectedly I found myself at a crossroads, one sign pointing to Argentina, the other Japan. Which way should I go? Even though my focus was Argentina, I found myself on a flight to Tokyo to begin married life in the Far East, instead of to Buenos Aires for a holiday in the sun.

My first impression arriving in Tokyo, the biggest city of the world, was I had landed on a different planet. Everything was strange and unfamiliar. Communication was impossible because I could not speak Japanese, let alone read any of the signs. I had every intention of learning the language, but never took lessons and only learned enough to go shopping, make polite greetings and direct a taxi. I found Tokyo a harsh, crowded city resembling a concrete jungle. In the early 70s it was a male-oriented society and foreigners were called *gaijins* or aliens, which increased the sense of being in another world. Everything was different and it took time to feel at ease in my new homeland. With my husband focused on his work, I was left to find my own way around and in the beginning it was a very lonely experience. I returned to the safety of my shell feeling homesick and missing my family and friends.

All we can do when facing a challenge is to dive deep into our own resources. Slowly I became used to living in a different world and learned to accept my new home and the Japanese culture that I found exceedingly beautiful and creative. Underneath the harshness, the Japanese have a deep connection with nature and spirituality that can be seen in the Shinto shrines, Buddhist temples and beautiful landscaped Zen gardens. The traditional Japanese houses stand side-by-side with modern office buildings, apartments and skyscrapers. It is a unique society that can shift easily from East to West in a moment. Despite the challenges of adjusting to my new homeland, I made the best of the new opportunity and learned traditional arts of Ikebana flower arranging and silk painting. We settled into an ex-pat lifestyle and made the most of travelling around the world visiting different countries on the flight routes between London and Tokyo and in the Far East.

We returned to England after five years and over the next 22 years my life unfolded with three children and a home to look after, as well as working part time. My dream to return to Argentina was put on hold until my eldest son, turned 18, who opened the door for me to go back.

Having heard about Argentina all his life, he decided to spend part of his gap year as a student teacher at St George's College North, in Buenos Aires. It was this event, which finally galvanised me to return. I arranged to visit him towards the end of his stay, taking with me my younger son who had completed his General Certificate School Examinations, one being Spanish. I thought this trip offered him an ideal opportunity to practise his newly acquired language skills, as well as see where his mother was born and raised. I planned our trip with an intense amount of excitement and trepidation, hardly daring to believe my dream was coming true and hoping nothing would get in the way this time.

In July 1993, we boarded our plane for the long-haul flight to Buenos Aires and I felt my excitement growing as we came into land at Ezeiza Airport. Thirty-three years after I had left, my feet once again stepped onto Argentine soil. Finally, my dream had become my reality. My son met us at the airport with his host and we drove into the centre of Buenos Aires along an old familiar highway passing sights that began to trigger memories of my childhood. I heard the distinctive sounds of the birds I had long forgotten and felt the walls of defensiveness I had built around me soften as I reconnected with the energy of my homeland. We arrived in the centre of Buenos Aires, the city of my birth. The noise and bustle of pedestrians and traffic, the buildings and shops is like any city except this was my city and something had changed. I was seeing them now through the eyes of an adult and not those of a child.

Heather had kindly arranged for us to stay with friends in the centre of town and we used their apartment as a base for our trip. We arrived in time for lunch and I had to recover my rusty Spanish language skills as our hosts spoke little English. I soon realised my schoolgirl vocabulary was limited and somehow needed to find the words to hold an adult conversation. Immersed in the language and the open-hearted welcome from our hosts helped me to relax, as well as enjoying a glass of *vino tinto,* and words I had long forgotten slowly began to return.

My excitement at finally being back in my beloved homeland built as we planned our stay. I was eager to show my sons where we had lived in Hurlingham and also visit Heather's family home at the Estancia La Esperanza near San Clemente, where we had spent our last few days in Argentina shortly before we left. The family no longer owned La Esperanza and Heather's parents and her brother, Donny, now lived across the road from the *estancia*. Donny invited us to stay and arranged for us to visit his parents and La Esperanza.

Andrew, Heather and Donny's younger brother, kindly drove us down to San Clemente the next day. We left the city and headed south across the *pampas*, the flat grasslands stretching to the horizon with nothing except trees, cattle, sheep and horses and windmills to interrupt the view. The sights and sounds, which had meant so much to me began to trigger the emotions of joy instead of the sorrow I had been holding onto ever since I had left. I thought about the happy times we had spent at La Esperanza, and how much I had missed seeing my friends since we had left the country. We arrived at Donny's house and later he drove us to visit La Esperanza. We stopped to open the gate at the entrance to the *estancia* and slowly drove through the *monte* where we had waited for my parents the day they never arrived. I could smell the scent of the eucalyptus trees wafting through the air and felt I was home at last. We approached the house and parked the car. We walked around the outside of the house and across the lawns towards the barns and corrals where the horses were kept. I stood at the gate looking out across the fields where we once rode our horses, galloping across the open land without a care in the world. It seemed a lifetime ago and yet in that moment I was a child feeling the freedom of riding across the open space with no fences or boundaries and uninterrupted views towards the horizon. We reminisced about our childhood and the fun we had had on our holidays when we stayed with the family. It was emotional and wonderful to be there again after so many years.

Our visit at an end we returned to Donny's house and he saddled up horses for us to ride. It felt wonderful being back in the saddle on an

Argentine horse after so long. I had done some riding in England and it wasn't the same. We rode through the open fields, the space affording a sense of peace and freedom I had not felt since I had left this beautiful land. This area of the camp is near the coast and a haven for wildlife and birds. A Mundo Marino, Sea World, has been established nearby with sea lions, orcas, penguins, walrus and dolphins entertaining visitors and helping to conserve the habitat of wildlife and sea creatures. Our visit came to an end all too soon and we returned to Buenos Aires by bus, passing flooded fields after days of heavy rain. It reminded me of our journeys to visit my uncle when it rained and we got stuck in the mud. Luckily we were on main roads and not at risk of being stranded.

The next day we took the train to Hurlingham, the trains hadn't changed as much as I had. We were meeting up with an old school friend who knew the present owner of our old house and had kindly arranged for us to visit. We alighted on the platform of Hurlingham railway station and met my friend and together we walked down the now paved road to my childhood home. It felt surreal to actually be there, as though I was in a waking dream. We arrived outside our house and rang the bell at the gate to announced our arrival. The voice behind the bell answered and the gate opened and I stepped once again into my childhood home. We walked down the garden path, no longer guarded by roses. The layout of the garden had changed and many of the trees had gone but the house was the same, although it looked smaller than I had remembered. I felt like *Alice in Wonderland* realising that I had grown in the intervening years. Memories and emotions filled my heart and mind as I walked around the garden, but we did not go inside the house, it no longer belonged to me. It was wonderful to have finally returned. I thanked my friend for organising our visit and asked her to convey my gratitude to the owner. I said a silent farewell to our old house and closed the gate on a chapter in my life.

We walked up the road, passed the house where Heather had lived and where we had played together almost every day. We crossed the main road and continued towards our old school, St Hilda's College, a short journey that we had taken daily on our bicycles. We arrived at the walled entrance and gates to the school and walked into the courtyard, where we had stood every morning singing the Argentine national anthem as the flag was raised about the school entrance. A member of staff met us and invited us to look around. We entered through the front door into the hallway. The school was closed for the winter holidays but I could hear the sound of schoolgirl chatter in my ears. We walked into the Assembly Hall where we had gathered every morning in our houses, and where ballet and Scottish dancing lessons had been held. At the far end was the stage where I had taken part in a dancing display, dressed as a solider girl. My art work had also been displayed on the walls in the Art Exhibition. Next to the Hall was the flight of stairs to the classrooms on the first floor. We walked up the stairs and I found my old classroom. I opened the door and remembered sitting at my desk. We had lessons in Spanish in the morning and lessons in English in the afternoon which was confusing, especially in Arithmetic. I remember the friends I made in this classroom and how lucky to have stayed in touch with many of them. We have remained close despite my leaving at a young age and many now live in England. I had recently been to an Old Girl's lunch in London organised by The St Hilda's College ex-Alumni United Kingdom which keeps us connected wherever we are in the world.

We wandered around the school and the gardens and then continued down memory lane to the road where Viola and Frank had lived. I was very close to my aunt and uncle and our family met up with them most days. Viola and Frank had an open house and friends were always popping in to say hello. They had a telephone, something we did not possess, and it was a treat to watch them use it! The house was a short walk from St Mark's Church, where I had been christened and my father had been a verger. A new hall had been built in the grounds which my mum had helped finance through fund raising with the WDA. We continued our walk towards the

Hurlingham Club, passed the nursery school I had attended and the shops where we brought bread and groceries. So many familiar places and it felt wonderful to be back in my hometown, but I was also sad because I felt I no longer belonged. I had moved on and had created a new life in England. I pushed aside my uncomfortable feeling of not belonging and focused on being in places which had meant so much to me. All that mattered was I was home again.

I also planned a visit to Jujuy and see where mum had grown up. Having heard so much about it, I wanted to connect with the home she had loved so deeply. We boarded a plane from Aeroparque, the city airport and flew north to San Pedro de Jujuy to stay with Richard and Caroline Leach at the Finca Los Lapachos. Richard is the grandson of Norman Leach, one of the founder members of Leach's Argentine Estates, the company where my grandfather, Ambrose, had worked and mum and dad had first met at the train station outside the *finca*. My parents had never taken us to visit Jujuy when I was a child and I was looking forward to finally seeing it for myself.

Richard and Caroline warmly welcomed us and I felt at home from the moment I arrived. They showed us round their beautiful colonial-style house built around a central courtyard with spacious rooms and high ceilings with fans for cooling the rooms in the summer heat. The house was surrounded by a veranda overlooking a wonderful tropical garden with trees, shrubs, flowers and an avenue of palm trees. It was mid-winter in the southern hemisphere and we enjoyed the warmth from log fires burning in the large stone fireplaces. Knowing our love of riding, Richard had horses saddled ready for our use and we enjoyed riding around the sugar cane fields, as my mother and my grandfather had done many years before.

Richard took us to visit the Ingenio La Esperanza in the nearby town of San Pedro which was still a working factory. It was fascinating to watch the sugar cane arrive in huge trucks and emptied onto conveyor belts, which dropped its contents into machines to be churned and pulped to eventually become the sugar filling the bowls on our tables. I felt the blood of my ancestors running through my veins as I followed the footsteps of my grandfather who walked the same floors many years before. I thought of mum and felt the magic and energy of this beautiful land in the foothills of the Andes. I could understand why she had loved it so much and the devastation she felt when she had to leave. I followed her early life, feeling more at home with every step I took.

Richard and Caroline took us on a drive into the Andes through the Humahuaca Valley on the road towards the Bolivian border. We drove through the majestic rainbow coloured mountains to the little village of Purmumarca in the valley known as the Siete Colores, seven colours. We entered another world belonging to the indigenous population who wear their traditional brightly coloured clothes and bowler hats. They earn their living weaving textiles and making coloured cloth into *ponchos,* jumpers, hats, gloves, socks, cushion covers and throws which were neatly laid out on tables around the village square. The mountainous area and the high altitude and rough terrain are only suitable for sure-footed animals, such as llamas and alpacas, which provide the wool for the vibrant coloured textiles and woven knitwear that makes this part of the world so distinctive and well known. I became the tourist in my own land and bought myself a *poncho* and scarves and hats to take home as gifts for the family.

We continued our drive up the valley to Tilcara, a name familiar from my mother's childhood where she and her family spent holidays to escape the intense heat in the summer. The small town is strategically placed overlooking the valley with the ruins of an Indian fort on top of a peak surrounded by giant cacti, which has not changed over the years. We walked around the ruins and I listened for the sound of the panpipes, the music that has haunted me ever since I first heard the distinct tones of the cane flutes. But the only panpipe music I heard came from market stalls selling CDs, sadly I saw no mystical shaman standing on the mountain playing his panpipes in the setting sun.

Our visit to Jujuy came to an end and we returned to Buenos Aires. The following day we flew north into the jungle to visit the Cataratas del Iguazu, the largest waterfall system in the world bordering Argentina and Brazil. We were greeted with a hot and humid tropical paradise with colourful plants and flowers, birds and animals. We stayed on the Argentine side of the falls and explored the pathways and walkways that meander around the perimeter of the cliffs marvelling at the magnificence of the largest fall, the Garganta del Diablo, Devil's Throat. Here, water pours over the sheer cliff in a never-ending torrent, creating beautiful rainbows in the sunlight from the rising mist. We took a boat ride to the base of the falls and gazed up at the sheer height of the cliff side, getting soaked despite our plastic *ponchos*. It was magical and mesmerizing to witness the power of nature and the beauty of Mother Earth.

Inspired by our experiences and all we had seen, we returned to Buenos Aires for our flight back to London. My heart was heavy with sadness despite the joy of returning as I knew there was nothing left for me in Argentina, only memories and ancestors buried in graveyards. I had returned to seek closure and there was no reason to go back again. I didn't recognise the sadness I felt was the voice of my heartbroken inner child who had deep emotional wounds that needed to be released and my healing journey had only just begun.

CHAPTER 21

MY HEALING JOURNEY UNFOLDS

We celebrated the arrival of the new Millennium and I felt the call to return to the land of my birth. In the intervening years my marriage had ended in divorce and I was now with a new partner. It felt right to introduce him and my daughter to Argentina. I planned a similar trip to the one I had made with the boys several years before to visit Heather's family in San Clemente, Richard and Caroline in Jujuy and friends in Hurlingham. We travelled out with Margaret and her husband, David, who were on their annual visit to family in La Cumbre in the Sierras de Cordoba and they suggested we join them for a few days on our way up to Jujuy. Margaret had lived down the road from us in Hurlingham and had been spending holidays in La Cumbre since she was a child. I had never been to La Cumbre and was looking forward to visiting a place I had heard so much about. After my mother passed away, I found a photograph of her parents taken at the La Cumbre Golf Club and realised this must have been where they were staying when they wrote about visiting the Cordoba hills in their war-time letters.

We were met at Ezeiza Airport by Heather who had arrived with her children for their summer holiday a few days earlier. We hired cars and courageously drove into Buenos Aires along Avenida 9 de Julio, the 9-lane highway that runs through the centre of the city and is the widest avenue in the world. Thankfully we survived the challenge of the midday traffic which made rush hour in London tame in comparison. We had booked our first night to stay at the Hurlingham Club, and Margaret, Heather and I had a St Hilda's Old Girls reunion to attend. A group of old girls getting together in any part of the world is always an excuse for a reunion. It was fun meeting friends I had not seen since I had left and we reconnected as though we had never been apart. The following morning we walked around Hurlingham and along the road where we used to live. We stood outside our house but we did not ring the bell to go inside.

Later that afternoon we drove down to San Clemente, together with Heather and her family. It was mid-summer and we enjoyed the beautiful weather and a quad bike ride along the wide sandy beach and celebrated the New Year into the early hours of dawn with Donny and his family. We visited La Esperanza again before returning to Buenos Aires to catch the overnight bus to La Cumbre. Luxury double-decker buses leave from Retiro bus station, the central hub of passenger road transport throughout Argentina, to all parts of the country, many travelling the long distances overnight. We left the camp at the height of the midday sun, in temperatures of 40 degrees Celsius, and we arrived at Retiro station ready for the cool air-conditioning on the bus. However, I had not prepared myself for the sudden drop in temperature and spent a chilly night wearing my sun hat to protect my head from the incessant blast of cold air. I felt the beginnings of a sore throat and by the time we arrived in La Cumbre, I could barely speak.

Margaret met us off the bus and took us to the chalet where we were staying and introduced us to her Argentine family and to the life and wonder of this small English enclave deep in the Argentine countryside.

The town of La Cumbre nestles in the Punilla Valley of the Sierras Chicas, in the province of Cordoba, 900 kilometres north-west of Buenos Aires. Situated at 1141 metres above sea level, La Cumbre took its name in 1892 as the last and highest stop on the old railway line from Cordoba. The disused railway station is now the Information and Art Centre, affording the talented artistic community an unusual venue for their shows and exhibitions. The town is a popular holiday centre for adventure sports, including mountain-biking, hiking and paragliding, as well as riding and golf. The warm sunshine and fresh mountain air offers an escape from the heat of the city and is the perfect place to restore the mind, body and spirit. It also affords the ideal environment for the recovery from ill health and in the past provided hospitals and convalescent homes for people suffering from tuberculosis and other chest conditions.

I walked the streets of La Cumbre feeling I was back in Hurlingham, the same style houses and bungalows behind high hedges, many with large gardens and swimming pools. We were introduced to people who had known our family when we lived in Hurlingham and remembered mum and dad with love and affection. Everyone was friendly and openhearted, making us feel at home even though we had only just arrived. Many of those we met shared similar stories of ancestors leaving their homelands in England, Ireland and other European countries more than a century before. Some had come out to work on the railways, others went into farming, like my grandfather. We were welcomed like long-lost friends, making new friends easily and reconnecting with those from childhood.

A lovely surprise was to meet my second-grade Spanish teacher who had taught me at St Hilda's and bought furniture from my parents when we left Hurlingham, forty years before, when she set up home as a young bride. We also met the family who had bought our house and they were still using the garden furniture they bought with the house forty years before! It was wonderful to be in a place where everything felt familiar making me feel at home. The days unravelled in synchronicity and spontaneity with invitations to coffee, lunches and tea parties. Tea at five o'clock is as revered an occasion as it is in England, apart from the time because the Argentines eat dinner late; nine o'clock is normal. One memorable invitation was to join the ladies of the Guild for tea after their final meeting of the year. I arrived to find a room filled with more than 30 women, all speaking Spanish to one another even though their native language was English. The quirkiness of Span-glish, a mixture of Spanish and English reminded me of how I loved everything about their way of life, which was so different to life in England.

One day Margaret's brother-in-law, Francois, took us on a trip into the mountains to meet a powerful crystal healer and shaman in his healing sanctuary overlooking the mystical Mount Uritorco. At 1949 metres, the mountain dominates the landscape and is the highest peak in the Sierras Chicas. With regular sightings of Unidentified Flying Objects and rumours of inter-dimensional portals and a city of light, it has an air of mystery. Capilla del Monte, the town at the foot of the mountain, attracts spiritual seekers in the same way as Glastonbury does in England. The shaman offered me healing for my chest cold, which he said was on the verge of developing into pneumonia as the tears of my broken heart started to heal. My wellbeing improved after the healing and he gave me some herbal mountain tea to aid the decongestion in my chest. We explored other local areas and went riding over the hills on horses that know how to navigate the steep terrain, a different experience to riding on the flat lands of the pampas.

I was beginning to love everything about this magical place and could easily have stayed forever. But all too soon we had to say farewell to our new friends and head north to Jujuy on another overnight bus journey. The bus broke down shortly before arriving and Richard came to rescue us, which thankfully avoided us having to wait for hours on the roadside before a replacement bus was found.

Richard and Caroline warmly welcomed us into their lovely home at Los Lapachos once again. We settled in and enjoyed daily rides around the estate, which was growing cotton as the factory had closed down sugar production since my previous visit. It was sad to see the abandoned factory with broken windows and rusty machinery lying around, an empty shell of its former glory when once it had been the heart of the community. It was another sign that it was time to move on. We were taken on another magical drive into the Humahuaca Valley, stopping off in Purmumarca and Tilcara to buy more *ponchos* and colourful knitwear. The majestic and colourful Andes afforded us another intense experience of joy and wonder.

We flew back to Buenos Aires to avoid another long-haul bus journey, spending our last few days in Hurlingham before we returned to London. Once again, I truly felt I no longer needed to go back, in my mind my wounds were healed. I had returned seeking closure for a second time and I was sure I could now let go.

The following year my partner and I were married. It was time to celebrate a new beginning. I hoped I could leave my past behind and move on with my life. At the time I was unaware of the deeper agenda going on and I was being called to heal the ancestral grief and heartbreak I was carrying and we would keep returning to Argentina until I had let the sadness go at the deepest level of my soul.

CHAPTER 22

THE HEALING CONTINUES

Four years later we were on another flight to Buenos Aires after receiving an invitation to visit friends at their holiday home in Punta del Este, Uruguay. We flew into Buenos Aires and stayed in a small hotel in the city centre. It takes me a few days to recover from a long-haul flight and settle into the energy of the vibrant and bustling city, which never sleeps. I loved walking the streets of the city and visiting the old familiar places. Calle Florida is one of the main pedestrian shopping streets and always busy with locals and tourists eager to pick up bargains from shops selling high-class fashion and leather goods of every shape and size, from shoes and boots, coats and jackets to handbags, wallets and belts. Strolling down Calle Florida is an important part of a visit to Buenos Aires, as is watching tango dancing in La Boca and Palermo, having a coffee and *medialuna*, croissant, in a downtown cafe and eating a delicious meal in one of the many restaurants on Puerto Madero, the old dockyard from where our ship sailed many years before, now refurbished into exclusive apartments, offices and restaurants.

We decided to venture out and booked a trip to the Tigre on the Delta del Parana, a popular weekend and holiday resort near the centre of Buenos Aires. A short train ride takes visitors to the quayside to embark on riverboats which take passengers around the delta, passing beautiful holiday homes that afford an ideal place to retire and retreat for the weekend and relax during the summer months. It has its own community with river boats delivering groceries and river buses taking children to school.

The following day we flew up to Jujuy from Aeroparque, the city airport adjacent to the Rio del la Plata, to spend a few days with Richard and Caroline at Los Lapachos who once again warmly welcomed us to their home. We settled into the magic of the ancestral homeland and enjoyed daily rides around the estate. Richard drove us to San Pedro and this time he took us to see Las Rosas, mum's childhood home. I had been looking forward to seeing the house having heard so much about it but, sadly the house was abandoned and neglected, the garden overgrown with vegetation, a relic of its former glory when it had once been vibrant with life and my mother's pride and joy. It held an air of nostalgia, as I imagined my grandmother taking afternoon tea on the veranda, waiting for my mother and my grandfather to return home from their ride around the sugar cane fields. I took photographs so I could show mum pictures of her childhood home, thinking she would like to see it again, but sadly they only brought tears to her eyes.

From Jujuy we flew to Montevideo in Uruguay, where we hired a car and drove the short distance to Punta del Este to stay with our friends, Margot and Michael. It was my first visit to Uruguay, apart from stopping at Montevideo on the boat trips to England, which never allowed time to see anything other than the city. On the drive to Punta del Este, we passed through beautiful rolling hills and open spaces, it had a very different feel to Argentina and I loved its soft vibrant energy. We arrived in Punta del Este and Margot and Michael warmly welcomed us to their beautiful seaside home. Margot and I have known each other since childhood as we used to play together when she visited her grandparents, who lived next door to us in Hurlingham.

We relaxed into easy conversation and I told them about a dream I had to open a healing centre. Over the years I had become interested in complementary and alternative therapies and had trained in Reiki, Emotional Freedom Techniques, Massage and the Aura-Soma Colour Care system. My idea was to have a retreat where people could stay and rejuvenate with a variety of treatments to help restore their balance and wellbeing. We thought it would be interesting to see what properties were available locally. Margot kindly introduced us to real estate agents who took us to see several wonderful places. Each one had the potential of fulfilling my dream, but one in particular drew me like a magnet. The property was a bungalow with a thatched roof resembling an English country cottage with a separate chalet for guests. It had a large garden and swimming pool overlooking open fields with a small lake in the middle of the property. Our idea was to divide our time in each country, an endless summer seemed perfect. We negotiated with the agents, although a purchase would be dependent on selling our house in England.

We returned home and put our house up for sale but the timing coincided with the start of the global collapse in the property market. After a year our house remained unsold and reluctantly, we decided it was not feasible to go ahead with the property in Uruguay. My dream had to remain a dream. I also reflected on why we were considering Uruguay. We were captivated by our first visit, yet I knew my heart belonged in Argentina. If we were seriously considering investing in a property, it should be in Argentina.

Two years later we returned to Argentina to join Margaret and David on a wine tasting tour to Mendoza they had organised for their Wine Group in Cheshire. They were happy for us to tag along and I looked forward to visiting parts of Argentina I had never been to before. We arrived a few days before the tour began and went to stay with Margaret and David in La Cumbre before we all returned to Buenos Aires, where the tour was to start. We were booked into Claridges Hotel where we met up with the rest of the group. We spent our first day on a Dia del Campo at a nearby *estancia* enjoying an *asado* and a ride even though it poured with rain the whole day. Luckily we had a spacious barn to shelter inside and we dried off in front of a large open fire. The sun returned the next day and we went on riverboat excursion to El Tigre for lunch and in the evening were entertained to a dinner and tango show. The next day we flew across the country to Mendoza, the centre of the wine producing area in the foothills of the Andes. Our tour was to visit some of the major local wine producers around Mendoza and San Rafael. The main grapes for the Argentine wines are Malbec, Merlot and Pinot Noir. Our visit began in San Rafael at the winery of Valentin Bianchi. From there we visited the wineries at O'Fournier and Bodega Salentein. We also visited Chandon, Weinart and Nieto Senitiner. Chandon produces a sparkling wine similar to champagne. It was fascinating seeing how the wine is produced and stored in wine cellars, some of which are adorned by beautiful works of art on the walls to enhance the flavour of the wine as it matures in barrels.

Margaret and David arranged a day trip to Aconcagua Provincial Park. Our bus stopped for us to admire the majestic presence of Mount Aconcagua before continuing higher into the Andes, climbing to 3,832 metres to visit the statue of Cristo Redentor, Christ the Redeemer of the Andes. The statue is located at the pass, coincidentally called La Cumbre, the highest point on the old road between Mendoza and Santiago de Chile and built to commemorate the peaceful resolution of border disputes between Argentina and Chile. It was a magical and memorable trip enhanced by the amazing organisational skills Margaret and David put into creating one of their unique Priceless Tours. The tour ended in La Cumbre and from there we returned to England with thoughts of maybe buying a property in Argentina uppermost in our minds.

CHAPTER 23

SUMMERS IN LA CUMBRE

Seven months later we were on another flight to Buenos Aires, the magnetic pull to keep returning was getting stronger, especially as our intention was to look for a property to buy where I could set up my healing centre. We took the overnight bus up to La Cumbre and rented a beautiful house belonging to Coco, Margaret's brother-in-law, situated on the hillside above the town with magnificent panoramic views across the valley and from where we sat every evening watching beautiful sunsets.

We settled into what was now a familiar place and contacted real estate agents to see what potential property was available to manifest a healing centre into reality. We viewed many beautiful places but none captured my imagination. The property in Uruguay. was the perfect place but in the wrong country. Our house was unsold which made us reflect that as much as the dream was inspiring, life was saying otherwise. We let go of the idea of buying a property and setting up a healing centre, but that wasn't to say our visits to La Cumbre were at an end. With all thoughts of investment out of our minds, we decided to rent instead of buy and made plans to return to La Cumbre the following year. Something kept drawing us back to this magical place.

The next year we booked a three-month stay at Francois' house along the road from Coco's house on the hill. Another beautiful property with a swimming pool on the mountainside, which provided wonderful views across the valley. We made full use of the summer and invited friends from England to come and visit us, which meant I took the overnight bus to Buenos Aires to meet them at the airport. It was fun introducing our friends to the vibrant and colourful city of my birth before catching the overnight bus to La Cumbre. We showed our friends around La Cumbre and had some magical moments together.

For the next three years we continued to fly south, like swallows migrating to escape the cold English winter. Each time we returned I breathed a sigh of relief, relaxed and entered a different space that wasn't only physical. I became myself where I felt at home. My roots connected to an energy which I had never found in England. I seemed to lose myself mid-Atlantic, arriving in Argentina connected to my inner being and disconnected when I arrived back in England. Perhaps it had something to do with a change of identity, as I left London on my British passport in my married name and arrived in Buenos Aires on my Argentine passport in my single name, Jeanine roughly translates to Juana. No wonder I felt lost. I tried to understand what made the difference, perhaps it was as simple as being in the land I loved and where I had been truly happy. Places hold memories and everywhere I went reminded me of my childhood which made sense why I felt happy and at peace in a place I had loved so deeply. Friendships grew with a sense of community and a feeling of belonging began to emerge, something I had never been able to find in England.

Each visit offered a deeper level of healing and I was guided to Andrea Garcia, a Vibrational Therapist, with a gift to connect with Spirit to help and support people on their spiritual journey for personal transformation, healing and empowerment. Andrea helped me to access the deeper story that lay beneath the heartbreak of being born in one land and living my life in another. It was a soul memory from another lifetime which is why it felt so deep. To become aware that my soul recreated a past-life experience in order to heal the past helped me to surrender and trust in a higher plan. Our souls evolve through challenges and I felt the truth of what Andrea told me. The concept of past lives and reincarnation has resonated with me since I had healing with Arthur, mum's healer friend from East Wittering, when I was a teenager. At the time I was having difficulties with my job which were connected with another past-life memory.

I surrendered to the agenda of my soul and was guided to help others. On each trip I took my Aura-Soma chakra set of bottles, containing the naturally extracted colours, essential oils and essences of plants, flowers and herbs. I set up a therapy room in each house we stayed in to help people connect with the vibration of colour to know themselves at a deeper level. I had recently learned a Colour Chakra massage technique unique to Aura-Soma using the oils and essences to release blocked energy in the seven major chakras in the body and was eager to share this deep and transformative massage with others. Margaret was my first client and she loved the massage so much she enthusiastically spread the word among her friends. Before long I had a diary filled with appointments. Some clients spoke Spanish which meant I had to shift my language skills to another level, a steep learning curve which improved my fluency dramatically.

Another avenue of colour opened up when Francois and his wife, Jill took us to the opening of Sala O'Campo, a new art gallery in town belonging to a well-known Argentine artist, Miguel O'Campo. Miguel used large canvas for his paintings and I was transfixed by the energy emanating from some of his works of art through the colour he used in his paintings. Francoise introduced us to Miguel and his wife, Susy, and I told them how his paintings made me feel. They were interested in my interpretation about the energy of colour and suggested I give a talk, as many people in La Cumbre are artists and would probably be fascinated to learn about the vibration of colour. I saw a new opportunity opening and said how much I loved their idea and boldly asked if could hold the talk in the Sala O'Campo! Miguel kindly agreed and we set a date for the following year.

We arrived back in La Cumbre the following summer and I arranged my talk at the Sala O'Campo. We sent out invitations and the evening arrived. I stood before an audience of talented artists with Miguel and Susy in the front row and began to talk about The Language of Colour and how we are attracted to colour and the message that can bring to us on all levels of our human experience. I felt energised and inspired by Miguel's beautiful works of art surrounding me and everyone was enthralled. Susy owns a gift shop in the town called *La Urraca* and told everyone who entered her shop about my work with colour. Soon I was inundated with requests for treatments and my healing practice expanded with daily appointments. Before long, I was working non-stop and memories of mum and her healing work flashed through my mind. I then realised I had created my healing centre in Argentina, but not in the way I had thought it would happen. Each year we returned to La Cumbre, I had clients waiting for me as soon as I arrived, the telephone rang and my healing work began.

I gave my initial talk on the Language of Colour in English with the intention to repeat it in Spanish the following year. I hosted a tea party and gave a similar talk in Spanish. I invited everyone we knew but was not expecting standing room only as friends and strangers came through the door. Pride of place was my Spanish teacher, who sat smiling at her pupil deliver a talk in Spanish. The nervous little girl I once was felt completely at ease as I spoke about my passion for healing and the magic of colour in my native language. I was standing in my truth and being myself in a place which felt like home. A magic moment I will always remember.

Each visit afforded a different experience of healing. Another avenue opened up through music and dance. Francois invited us for a drive to visit a friend of his, Daniel, at the Posada Puerta del Cielo, a healing retreat in Ongamira, deep in the mountains in the foothills of Mount Uritorco. Daniel and his partner, Marisa Cheb Terrab, a Yoga and 5 Rhythms dance teacher, have created a beautiful sanctuary surrounded by nature where they hold residential workshops on Yoga and 5 Rhythms. 5 Rhythms is a dance movement devised by Gabrielle Roth in the late 1970s, connecting to the natural rhythms in the body: flowing; staccato; chaos; lyrical; and stillness. My inner child loved to dance and I signed up for a workshop and Margaret and a new friend, Heather, joined me. In the beginning it was difficult to relax until I let go of the belief that *I cannot dance.* I closed my eyes and dropped into my heart surrendering to the music. For hour after hour the music played and we kept dancing. I allowed my body to move in whichever way it needed to release the pain and restrictions of not being myself. By the end of the workshop, I felt transformed and renewed in mind body and spirit. It was amazing to experience how the power of music can release deep seated emotions in ways that are beyond words.

We left La Cumbre and spent another few days in Buenos Aires before returning to London. My intention was to visit St John's Pro-Cathedral, the church where my parents were married. The impressive building stands on Calle 25 de Mayo, a few blocks from where we were staying at Hotel Claridges. We walked into the church and were met by a kind verger who came to greet us. I explained my mission and he took us into a small room, which contained the safe filled with Registers. He opened the door of the safe and began bringing each one out and carefully placing them on a nearby table. Finally, he found the one he was looking for, the Marriage Register for 1941, old and dusty at the bottom of the pile. He laid it on the table, blowing the dust off the cover. He slowly opened the book and turned the thin, fragile pages until he found the entry we were looking for:

16th April 1941 - Joan Constance Alexander married Maurice Neville Brownrigg.

I read the entry written in permanent ink, evidence my parents had married in that church 70 years before. It felt surreal and in that moment I recognised my life had begun. I walked back into the church imagining my mother arriving at the church in her beautiful wedding gown on the arm of her father. I wondered what she must have felt as young bride on her wedding day, marrying the man she loved and with my father standing at the altar waiting to greet the woman he had chosen to be his wife. I thought of their parents, Ambrose and Lillian, and Gerald and Maud, as they witnessed the love of the young couple and the joining of their families, surrounded by their friends and loved ones. It was a moment to treasure as much for them as it was for me.

My father's office was on Avenida de Mayo and we walked up the street to find the building where he worked. I stood outside the ornate front door looking up at the balcony where we used to stand overlooking the street remembering the excitement I felt at the thought of visiting him in his office. I could see the entrance hall with its black and white tiled floor and the lift with sliding metal doors that took us to the first floor. It was a short walk into his office where we found him sitting behind a large wooden desk. It was a treat to go to town on the train, a journey he made every day. He returned home at bedtime and came to say goodnight. I always asked him the same question, *"What did you do today, Daddy?"* He sat on my bed and told me about the friends he met for lunch and then read to me, my favourite bedtime story was *Haiwatha*.

Back in the present world, a few blocks away from dad's office we discovered the Cafe Tortoni, the epitome of an Argentine cafe from a time gone by. The Cafe was opened by a French immigrant in 1858 and frequented by the rich and famous, artists and painters, business men and politicians, who met to discuss the latest crisis or pass the time of day playing billiards or cards and dance the tango. Time stands still when you walk into the Cafe with glistening chandeliers hanging from an elaborately decorated ceiling and wood panelled walls covered in paintings and other works of art reminiscent of a bygone era. Efficient waiters move quickly between the tightly packed tables serving their customers. It is a popular place to enjoy a *cafe con leche,* a glass of *vino tinto* and *tostados de jamon y queso* or *sandwich de miga,* ham and cheese wafer-thin toasted sandwiches and *tortas, medialunas y alfajores,* cakes, croissants and pastries filled with *dulce de leche,* listening to the passionate music of the tango. I wondered if this was where dad had lunch with his friends when he worked up the street. I think it probably was his favourite place to meet.

There was so much to see and so many memories making it harder each time to say goodbye.

CHAPTER 24

THE JOURNEY ENDS

We loved our annual migration to Argentina to escape the English winter and planned our trip for early 2012 to share a house with Margaret and David to coincide with their holiday plans. As we were planning our trip, I received an email from Ann Brownrigg introducing me to a second cousin, Suzanne Paget, who lives in Devon, who I had not heard about before. Ann told me Suzanne's grandmother was Evelyn Hoyle, sister to my grandmother, Maud, which came as a surprise as I wasn't aware my grandmother had a sister. It was exciting to hear about another member of the family, especially as I was writing a book about my ancestors. I contacted Suzanne, who was keen to hear my story as she likewise had little information about her great aunt Maud's family. A new branch of the family tree opened up for us both.

It was lovely to talk to Suzanne and learn about Maud and Eveyln and their life in New Zealand before they moved to Argentina. I had known my grandmother was born in New Zealand and her father was from Scotland but had no other information about her family. Suzanne told me Maud and Evelyn's uncle was Elsdon Best (1856-1931), who was an ethnographer and had made valuable contributions to the study of the Maori. I told Suzanne about our upcoming visit to Argentina and she asked me if I could find the grave of her grandmother, who had died at a relatively young age from tuberculosis and was buried in Cordoba. I said I would do my best as La Cumbre is situated in the province of Cordoba, but with no other information it would be like looking for a needle in a haystack.

We arrived in La Cumbre in February and hosted a *vino y empanada* party which gave me the opportunity of asking friends where I could begin my search. It was suggested I contact Peggy James, who held the records of the Anglo-Argentines buried in the Anglican cemeteries in the area. Peggy lived up the road from where we were staying and the following day I walked round to see her. She was fascinated by my request and went to find her records but could find no trace of my great aunt. However, she offered to take me to the nearby town of Capilla del Monte to ask at the Records Department of the local Municipal Office. The following day, her driver took us to Capilla and we made enquires at the Records Department. I left my great aunt's name with the clerk and was asked to call back in a few days. On our way back we went to the local cemetery and asked the caretaker if he would kindly look through his registers. Unfortunately, his search found no trace of Evelyn Hoyle and we returned to La Cumbre wondering where to go next. Peggy said she would look through her records again in case she had missed any and suggested I call her later in the afternoon. When I rang Peggy, she excitedly told me she had located Evelyn's grave, which was No 27 in the Anglican Cemetery in Calle Cordoba in La Cumbre! She said that when I spelled my great aunt's name at the Records Office she realised she had misheard Evelyn's surname which made her look again. We were astonished and delighted to know she had been found.

The next day Peggy took me to the Anglican Cemetery and we found the last resting place of my great aunt Evelyn. I placed flowers on her grave, grateful for the remarkable way we had been drawn together. It was extraordinary to connect with a member of my family who I had only heard about a few months previously, even more realising I had been coming to La Cumbre for so many years without knowing of her existence. It was beyond my mind to understand and wondered if this was another reason I had to keep going back. We have not returned to La Cumbre since then, as though the mission has been completed. Another gift is knowing I have family in Santa Fe, who I hope to meet one day, instead of only ancestors in graveyards.

The magic continued when Margaret and I signed up for a Soul Motion dance workshop at the Posada Puerto del Cielo in Ongamira. Soul Motion is a conscious dance practice created by Vinn Arjuna Marti. The workshop was led by Yukiko Amaya, another inspiring dance teacher. It was wonderful to return to the Puerta del Cielo and enjoy the healing sanctuary in the mountains. My opening heart took me deeper as I allowed my body to release more layers of restrictions and limited beliefs, another emotional and transformation experience. At the end of the workshop we took a ride to the top of Colchiqui, the sacred mountain of the Comechingone Indians, who once lived in Ongamira until they were persecuted and annihilated by the conquistadors who ravaged the land of its native people. We rode our horses along narrow tracks up to the peak at a height of 1500 metres, allowing our sure-footed ponies to effortlessly carry us up the mountainside. When we reached the peak, we dismounted and watched condors gliding on thermal currents and flying back to their nests precariously balanced on the rock face. It was magic to observe these magnificent birds in flight, with their distinctive ruff of white feathers around their necks and large wingspans with finger feathers at their wingtips, showing us how to let go and be taken on the wind. We rode back in the setting sun, my awakened heart filled with joy and love, feeling connected to the beauty and wonder of the land.

A few days later I found myself on the top of another mountain. We had decided to attempt a climb to the top of Mount Uritorco, which at 1949 metres was higher than Colchiqui. This time it would be up to me, and not my horse, to get me there and would be a test of physical endurance beyond anything I had experienced before. It was my husband who had a strong desire to climb the mountain and over the years had mentioned we should attempt the climb one day. It seemed the day had arrived and we enlisted the help of Francois, who had been climbing Uritorco for many years. With his support and guidance, I knew we would be in safe hands.

The thought of climbing to the summit of the tallest peak in the Sierras Grandes with its reputation of magic and mystery filled me with doubt as to whether I could make it or might fail in the attempt. The closest I had been to the top of a mountain before Colchiqui had been at Machu Picchu in Peru, the famous lost city of the Incas hidden in the Andes. Machu Picchu is situated at 2430 metres and we had taken a train from Cuzco to Agua Calientes, the village at the base of the mountain and a bus to the entrance of the national park, needing only a gentle stroll to reach the summit. Climbing to Mount Uritorco was not going to be an easy stroll in the park, I knew I would have to dig deep and take it one step at a time.

Francois picked us up early one morning and we drove to Capilla del Monte, the town nestling at the base of Uritorco, from where we began our climb. We left the car and with back packs filled with hats, water, snacks and sun cream, we walked across the river on a swing bridge to reach the start of our mountain trek. It was relatively cool in the fresh mountain air and the initial trail was easy, gently climbing in a winding path which took us round in circles as the trail led us higher and higher. We walked slowly, stopping in places for a drink where a convenient rock provided a welcome seat to rest. Cloud covered the sky and once the sun broke through, the temperatures started to rise.

We followed the path, Francois taking us on what was for him a familiar route; he usually reached the summit in two hours. We had been walking that long and not yet reached half way. Our pace was steady to allow our bodies to get used to the climb. The path took us deep into the mountains, the scenery was magnificent and we eagerly looked for condors. Eventually, we arrived a waterfall with a large rock pool and sat down to rest and drink from the crystal-clear mountain water, allowing the warmth of the sun to relax our weary muscles and bones. The path continued over the rocks to reach the other side of the pool. We were at a height of around 1500 meters and my husband decided he had reached the limit of his endurance and would not continue any further. He turned back down the mountain path to wait for us at the base.

Francois and I carefully climbed across the rocks to reach the path towards the summit. We arrived at the next station where an emergency crew have oxygen and first aid for those in need of assistance. We continued along the path and reached a plateau covered with waving grass and yellow flowers. We sat down in the grass amongst the flowers to rest our tired bodies and looked across the mountains and the wonderful view of the valley below. Refreshed from our short rest, we continued along the path, which began to take us on a steeper climb. We had reached the hardest part of the trek where the path gives way to rocks and stones and every step has to be taken with care. I was feeling the not-so-fit aspect of my physical fitness and my pace slowed. I did not look backwards, only onwards and upwards as my gaze reached higher and higher towards my goal.

Eventually after six hours, we reached the summit, exhausted and exhilarated after our climb. I had used up every atom of strength and was grateful and overjoyed my body had taken me to the top of the mountain. The strong wind gusted and whistled noisily around us as we stood together looking out across the mountains towards the distant horizon. As if on cue, a condor flew passed on the thermal current only a few metres away to acknowledge our achievement. We stood in awe watching this magnificent bird flying so close we could almost reach out and touch it's wings. A rich reward for making it to the top and another magic moment I will never forget.

We took time to rest and enjoy the magnificent views across the open countryside. I reflected on my climb up the mountain acknowledging how hard and challenging it had been and feeling a sense of achievement I had reached the summit. It reminded me of my life's journey and the challenges I had overcome and how each moment had led me to this moment of standing on top of a mountain. I felt immense gratitude for the opportunities that had brought me here, realising the journey is as important as reaching the destination. Francois and I slowly began our climb down the mountain, which I found harder than the climb up, perhaps because I was exhausted. I needed every ounce of energy to make it back to base. My husband was waiting for us at the cafe to welcome us back and we enjoyed a celebratory meal to restore and rejuvenate our exhilarated minds and tired bodies.

We booked to stay on an *estancia* high in the mountains before we returned home. The land had been ravaged by fire six months before after the dry winter and it was astonishing to see the fields restored with lush green pasture after the devastation. We rode every day, rounded up horses in a corral, enjoyed picnics by the river, swam in a lake and attempted to play polo. It was a relaxing and restorative end to an intense and emotional trip.

This was to be the grand finale of our summer holidays in Argentina as circumstances prevented us from returning the following year. I had to find a way to keep my spirits high through the depths of an English winter and I was drawn to connect to my creative spirit. I went back to the notes I made about mum and my conscious writing journey began and *Pioneering Spirit* slowly emerged into form.

CHAPTER 25

FOLLOWING THE ANCESTRAL TRAIL

I may not have returned to Argentina since 2012, but my ancestral search continued unabated. I had a wealth of information about the Brownrigg ancestors and it was time to connect with my Irish roots. In August 2016 my daughter and I flew to Dublin. I hired a car and we drove south towards Kilkenny. I booked an apartment in a wonderful old abbey located near to towns in the counties of Carlow, Wexford and Wicklow, where my great grandparents, Robert Graham and Amelia Brownrigg had lived.

Ann Brownrigg introduced me to Glascott Symes, a distant relation through the marriage of Robert and Amelia's daughter, Haddasa Cordelia, to Richard Henry Symes in 1880. Glascott kindly invited us to his lovely home near Durrow, where we studied a family tree as long as their extensive dining room table. Names I had never heard of came into our conversation as my understanding of my family expanded and I began to see a picture of the life my ancestors had experienced from the Civil War in England to the invasions, rebellions, uprisings and famines in Ireland. The Great Irish Famine, between 1845 and 1850 halved the population through death and mass migration. It was easy to understand why my grandfather had decided to migrate, along with so many of his generation as the prospect of a new life in another country away from the troubled homelands must have been compelling.

I was eager to visit the towns and areas that connected with the family roots and Glascott kindly offered to be our guide. Before we set off on the ancestral trail, my daughter and I drove to Lough Gur, a sacred lake near Holycross in County Limerick, which I had read about in a book I found in my mother's library, called *Mystical Britain and Ireland*. I felt drawn to visit this mystical lake with its myths and legend of enchantment about a hero rising from the lake on a white horse. I could feel the magic of the lake as we sat on the grass looking across the calm, blue water in the afternoon sun. I thought about the mystical lake I wrote about in *The White Horse* story which I had written before I had read about Lough Gur, wondering if my imagination had connected me to the spirit of my Irish ancestors.

We bought postcards from the shop in the Visitor's Centre and the lady behind the counter told us of an ancient stone circle nearby, which we stopped to visit before continuing our drive to Limerick. The Lough Gur Stone Circle is the oldest and largest stone circle in Ireland, believed to be over 4.000 years old and excavations have revealed evidence of Neolithic pottery. There were no other visitors when we arrived. We walked towards the circle of 113 standing stones, some up to 2.8m high covering a diameter of 150 feet, and saw four cows grazing inside the centre who filed out one behind the other as we stepped inside. We walked around the inside of the circle and found the healing stone, the largest standing stone. I stood against the stone and asked for healing of my ancestors thanking them for guiding us to this sacred space. I walked through the centre of the circle, wondering why it had been built in this particular place, perhaps the ancients could sense the energy of nearby Lough Gur. We walked out of the circle and the four cows stepped back inside. We returned to our car and three other cars arrived. It really did seem as though we had been given the space to be there on our own.

The next day we set off on our ancestral treasure trail with Glascott as our guide. We began in Bunclody, where my grandfather, Gerald Worthington Brownrigg, was born. At the time the town was called Newtownbarry, the name was changed in 1950. We found St Paul's Church in Kildavin and searched the gravestones in the small graveyard, but found none with a Brownrigg name carved into the headstones. We were unsure where else to look. Glascott asked a passerby and was directed to a lady in her nineties who lived on the outskirts of the town who we were told may be able to help with our search. We followed the directions and found the lady who kindly directed us to Kilrush, saying it was where many of the Brownriggs were buried.

We drove along the narrow country lanes and arrived at the village of Kilrush. We found the small stone church dedicated to St Brigid, surrounded by an old graveyard. There was a new graveyard on the opposite side of the road. We walked around the old graveyard and in one corner found a number of headstones carved with the name Brownrigg: William, Elizabeth, Henry, George, Jacob, Jane, Mary, Frank, Emily, Margaret and Thomas. By the dates, it was possible to see that some died as infants and young children. The oldest inscription was dated 1883, which was after my great grandfather had left the parish, which he served between 1868-1875. We walked across to the new graveyard and found a recent headstone dated 2013, which showed descendants continued to live in the area. Several names on the headstones were followed by the name of the house and town where they had lived, Newtownbarry, Graiguemore, Croneybrook, and Castlequarter. I knew Robert Graham had brothers called, William, George and Frank but the same names have been used through each generation, and it was not possible to be certain that of our family ancestors lay buried in the churchyard.

We left Kilrush and drove passed a house called Graiguemore. I felt compelled to stop and knock on the door and ask the owner if he was relative. Unfortunately he wasn't a descendant but said he had met with a Brownrigg the week before! He told us the Brownrigg family had left Graiguemore House and suggested we visit a Canon in Bunclody, who might be able to help. With the next clue on our treasure trail, we retraced our steps to Bunclody. On the way we passed a stonewall at the entrance to a long drive. The name Graiguemore House was carved in the wall. This could have been the ancestral home but knowing the family no longer lived there, decided not to enquire within.

We arrived back in Bunclody and found the Canon, who kindly invited us into his home. He told us there was a Roman Catholic Bishop, Abraham Brownrigg (1836-1928), who was a cousin of Robert Graham Brownrigg and had visited Kildavin School. It appeared that Robert Graham wasn't the only member of the family to have entered the Church and I later discovered his brother Francis (1818-1889) was ordained in 1848, as well as another brother, Thomas Richard (1821-1869), who had officiated at the marriage of Robert Graham and Amelia Worthington at St Jude's Church in Southsea, Hampshire. The Reverend Thomas Richard Brownrigg was the first incumbent of St Judes and his picture hangs on a wall inside the church.

We thanked the Canon for his help and continued our drive along the narrow country roads towards Tinahely, in County Wicklow, passing the ruins of the church in Crosspatrick, where my great grandfather had served (1877-85). Glascott had arranged for us to visit another ancestral family home, near Wingfield in County Wexford, now owned by a friend, which had belonged to the Henry Brownrigg line and passed to the Symes family through marriage. The original house was destroyed by fire during the Rebellion in 1798 and the present house was once the steward's house. It is possible that this was the area where Giles Brownrigg settled when he first arrived in Ireland in 1685. Our visit at an end we said farewell to our host thanking him for his hospitality. We headed back to Kilkenny stopping to visit the new church at Crosspatrick, where we found more Brownrigg graves. Our adventure at an end we thanked Glascott for his help and guidance and drove back to our abbey after a memorable day following the ancestral trail.

The next day we continued our research and visited Camolin in County Wexford, a town on the road from Enniscorthy to Wicklow, where Ann had told me my great great grandparents, Robert and Elizabeth, Robert Graham's parents, were buried in the churchyard of St. Catherine's Church. My great great grandfather, Robert Henry Brownrigg, lived at Norris Mount, near Camolin and married Elizabeth Graham. We found St Catherine's Church and walked around the graveyard trying to read the inscriptions on the old graves. At the back of the churchyard we found a large stone tablet under the trees with an inscription "in sacred memory of Robert Brownrigg, Esq of Norris Mount, Eliza his wife, eldest son Henry Bourke Brownrigg, Esq. JP and the Revd. Francis Brownrigg." Robert Brownrigg died in 1856, Eliza in 1866, Henry in 1869 and Francis in 1889. My connection to the ancestors expanded into another generation, I felt deep love for them all and placed a plant on the tablet in honour of their memory.

We left the ancestors and drove back towards Kilkenny, passing a sign to Norris Mount. I was tempted to continue our treasure trail but time did not allow us further research. It was our last evening in Ireland and we had a dinner date with Glascott and his wife, Adrienne, to thank them for their kindness and hospitality.

The following morning we said farewell to the abbey and drove back towards Dublin, with one more visit to make before we went to the airport. I wanted to find Robert and Amelia's grave in St Nahi's Church in Dundrum, on the outskirts of Dublin, The ancient churchyard has 1200 graves, fortunately we had a photograph Ann had emailed which she had taken on an earlier visit to Ireland which helped locate their graves with relative ease. Their adjoining headstones stood side by side, one fallen an angle but it was possible to read the inscriptions dedicated to my great grandparents. I stood in front of their final resting place and thanked their spirits for guiding us on our ancestral trail and placed a plant on their graves in loving memory. I felt my mission was complete. We turned and walked away and left the ancestors to their world.

CHAPTER 26

HEALING MY ANCESTRAL LEGACY

My personal journey, as I uncovered my ancestral past during the writing of this book, has been profound, transformative and unexpected. What began as my mother's simple request to write her memoir expanded into my own journey through my ancestors when I began to notice similar patterns emerging, which I recognised in my life. Diving into the past and uncovering what might lie hidden in my unconscious was totally unfamiliar to me with an inherited pattern of burying my emotions. I was shy and uncommunicative as a child and usually said *"I am fine"* if anyone asked me how I was doing. I was unable to express how I truly felt without dissolving into tears and was often asked why I always looked so sad, which I hotly denied not recognising my body language was speaking louder than my words. Not being honest how I was feeling was the only way I could cope and this habit has followed me most of my life, until I recognised it and began to let it go. As I released the blocks in my communication, I felt more comfortable being honest about how I was feeling. Writing has given me the opportunity to open the door to my heart as it has helped me dive deeper into my emotions. Expressing them on the page has been a step towards letting them go.

I had no way of knowing that by fulfilling my mother's last wishes, I would be thrust into my ancestral legacy. It has been a profound revelation to understand I carried the emotional wounds from my ancestors. As I reconnected with the heartbreak I felt when I left Argentina, I unconsciously connected with our ancestral wounds which up until then I felt were only mine. I do not believe my mother gave herself the opportunity to release her emotional wounds because her focus was on healing other people. However, when she no longer focused on others, she began to remember many of her experiences and connected with the emotions which had lain deeply buried inside her. The reality is however hard we try to bury our emotions and deny their existence, they remain lodged in our energy system until we have the courage and willingness to let them go.

My healing journey unfolded as I followed the ancestral footsteps of my forefathers to create a timeline from past to present and back again. The deeper I dived deeper into our family story, the more light I shone on my past seeing similarities in my own life. I stood back and saw my experiences through the eyes of my ancestors interweaving with each other, like threads in a tapestry interconnecting through patterns, beliefs, habits and behaviours. I realised it was the ancestors who held the key to identifying the deep emotional wounds which had continued to be passed down successive generations. My mother's simple request had opened Pandora's Box to heal myself and our family tree. During her life, she helped me to understand myself and in her death she continued to do so. Through healing myself and letting go of the sadness and grief, I had unconsciously being healing the ancestral timeline.

I inherited the pioneering spirit of my forefathers who left their homelands of origin in the 1600s to seek their fortunes in a new land. Successive generations of my paternal ancestors continued this pattern of being born in one land and taken to live in another. I now realise the heartbreak I felt leaving Argentina when I was ten years old wasn't only mine, but part of my inheritance from generations of ancestors leaving their homelands. The grief of leaving a place of belonging, the sadness caused by the separation from family and friends left behind and familiar places goes deep into our psyche. As the pattern continues through each generation, another layer is added until eventually someone becomes aware of them and can chose to let them go. While moving to another land was exciting and adventurous, I also felt the sadness, grief and longing to return to a place I loved, together with a feeling of not belonging and insecurity in my new homeland where I found it hard to feel accepted. At my first school in England, I was trying to make new friends, telling them about my life in Argentina but they soon became bored replying, *"Can't you talk about anything else, except Argentina?"* The answer was I didn't know what else to talk about and so I stopped talking, which made me feel isolated and alone. I now recognise the deep inner trauma this created as I denied myself in order to be accepted by others.

A profound release of this memory happened unexpectedly when I was driving through the town where we first lived in England. I felt compelled to find our old house and the school down the road I attended aged ten. As I turned into the lane, I saw our house and remembered living there as if it was yesterday. I continued down the road and came to the entrance of my old school and pulled into the drive to allow another car to pass in the narrow lane. Instinct made me drive through the school gates and not back into the lane. I wasn't sure why I was there as I walked towards the entrance and rang the bell at Reception. A lady appeared from an adjoining office and I told her I was an old pupil. She asked me if I would like to look round the school and she opened a door to my past. I walked along a corridor that lead to the dining room. I stepped inside and remembered having to eat a bowl of stewed gooseberries, which I realised I did not like after the first mouthful. We had to leave a clean plate and I was the last child to leave the dining room and have disliked gooseberries ever since. I walked into the hall where we gathered for morning assembly and where we took our exams. There was a stage at the far end and I remembered being the understudy in a play for the main role. I took part in all the rehearsals and can remember some of the lines, but didn't get to perform on the night. I looked around the room and suddenly felt an overwhelming sense of sadness as I recognised this was where I stopped being true to myself, for in the eyes of my ten year old child, I wasn't good enough or valued for being myself and I needed to change to please others in order to be accepted. Years of repressed tears started to flow as I connected to the long-buried pain of my inner child with compassion for myself as I had no way of knowing it would affect me all my life. I continued my tour and found my old classroom where I had sat as quiet as a mouse, without raising my hand because I had nothing to say. It seemed so much smaller than I had remembered but still held the memories. The emotions which came up as I continued walking around the school were intense and revealing. I had not expected to be taken back to my childhood in such a powerful way and left in a daze with the realisation I had spent a lifetime trying to undo the damage from the choice I had made 45 years before. I also realised closing my heart blocked my creativity and I struggled to find inspiration in my artwork and writing that had once flowed so freely. I was no longer being authentic and had lost connection to my true self and the source of my creativity.

I left the school and started driving home but with so many thoughts coming up, I needed to find somewhere to stop and process all that had happened. I saw a sign to a nature reserve. I walked towards a lake and sat on the water's edge to reflect on my sudden realisations. I watched a mother swan and her seven cygnets swim passed and was reminded of the story of *The Ugly Duckling* who only revealed his beauty when he realised he was a swan. Perhaps they were giving me a message about being true to myself. I heard the sound of children and a little girl and boy ran down to the water's edge and began prodding the water with sticks. Suddenly the little girl turned round and saw me. "Oh," she said, "I thought you were a little girl!" She had no way of knowing the truth of her words, for in that moment I was a little girl.

It was as I wrote about my mother's experience when she was sent to boarding school in England aged 14 and was so unhappy she ended up with pneumonia and nearly died that I realised I was not alone and she had felt the same way I did. Being a child from another land talking with a funny accent who has nothing in common with the other children is not unique to my mother and me. It happens to children across the world who are taken to live in a new land. We all want a sense of belonging to make us feel accepted and at home. Neither my mother nor I felt that in England which added another layer to our sadness. We longed to return to the place where we once felt truly happy. Even though my mother was born in London and returned to live in England, I am not sure she felt she belonged in England. Perhaps she always had a sense of restlessness and consequently filled her days with busyness as a distraction. I now wonder whether my grandmother, Lillian, felt she belonged in Argentina or whether my grandmother Maud and my great aunt, Evelyn, felt they belonged in Argentina or my great grandmother, Amelia, belonged in Ireland. They had all left the lands of their birth to move across the oceans to live in another land and may well have felt homesick for the family and friends they left behind.

It never occurred to me before writing this story that when I got married and went to live in Japan, I had followed in the footsteps of my grandmother and great grandmother who had done the same generations before. We had left the shores of England and travelled to a foreign country away from family and friends. We had willingly left the security and comfort of our homes and followed our beloveds to another land, as women were expected to do in those days. However, it left us with deep wounds of heartache from the separation from homes and family buried in our cellular memories. I had felt isolated and alone, cut off from friends and family, desperately homesick and wanting to go home. I did express how I felt, but I never thought of leaving. I made the best of it and had to adjust to my new life, as I am sure my grandmothers had done. I even wonder if they had the courage to express how they felt and what their husbands would have said to them. I doubt if they would have agreed to leave their jobs and return to England, expecting their wives to accept their new life without complaint, leaving them burying their feelings as there was nothing they could do to change the situation and they had to accept the life they had chosen.

My experience in Japan highlighted the challenges of adjusting to a new life in a foreign country without the support of family and friends. Communication has improved over the generations and now mobile telephones and the Internet enable us to stay in touch with each other wherever we are in the world and we can feel connected even when living apart from our loved ones. Not only has communication changed, but also the ease of transport. Ocean liners are now used for cruising and relaxation, rather than long-distant voyages and air travel is as common as catching a bus or a train taking us across the world in a matter of hours rather than weeks.

As I noticed familial patterns emerging, I began to wonder: whose life am I leading, mine, or my ancestors? Are we merely a sum of the totality of our family because we cannot separate one generation from another, despite the differences that seem apparent on the surface? Underneath in our collective unconscious it would appear we continue to play out uncompleted tasks and roles established by our ancestral lineage. This is expressed in common themes, likes and dislikes, patterns of behaviour, choice of partner, lifestyles, skills, natural gifts and talents. Yet, when we realise we are like our parents or grandparents, we are surprised as if it is a totally new concept!

CHAPTER 27

INNER HEALING

The level at which we heal is equal to the level we are willing to shine a light into our shadows and let go of the past. We can stay at the level of the mind believing we are victims of our genetic inheritance and there is nothing we can do or we can dive into our hearts and heal at the deepest level of our soul. My healing journey has shown me how my ancestral legacy of belief and behaviour passed on within my cellular memory and DNA. Scientific research into the study of epigenetics has identified how genes change their expression by responding to information in their environment. Does this challenge the belief we are victims of our genes and have to carry our ancestral baggage forever? Or can we accept we can affect the structure within our genetic makeup by changing our beliefs and behaviours and be willing to let them go. If we can change our default programme and create a life in alignment with who we truly are, we can let go of our collective belief that says we are victims of our inheritance.

We have to take responsibility for ourselves in order to liberate ourselves from the ties that bind us to our past. An essential part of liberating ourselves is the need to identify and release the emotions connected to the beliefs and behaviours that have led to our experiences. It is not only the physical attributes we inherit, but also the unconscious beliefs and emotions that remain unresolved throughout the generations. It is these which impact our lives, our overall health and wellbeing. We tend to think of inheritance in forms of wealth, yet we inherit far more than merely looks and material possessions. I inherited little in the way of financial wealth and material possession, but received an abundance of deeply buried emotions of sadness, sorrow, and heartbreak.

We incarnate into physical form to experience life through our emotions which underlay our reality. Our energy systems become blocked from unconscious emotions and create pain in our physical body. With the energy of heartbreak in our family story, I began to wonder if this was contributing to the migraines and headaches which affected my mother and her mother and from which I also suffer. My mother made references in her war-time letters about her ailing mother and I remember mum spending days in bed holding her head in pain. Pain is a message from the body to get our attention and while it is easier to reach for pain relief to alleviate the discomfort, having the courage and willingness to listen to the message underlying the pain offers an opportunity to heal at a deeper level. Whether or not my mother was able to understand the message behind her migraines, she seemed unable to connect with her emotions until she stopped focusing on the needs of others. Her unwillingness to express her emotions showed me the importance of expressing them, even though I spent my early years denying how I truly felt. When we repress our emotions, we carry the weight of the world on our shoulders. Once we let the emotions go, we feel lighter as our energy changes at a cellular level which raises our vibration and releases patterns trapped in our DNA. We label emotions as positive or negative without realising negative thoughts based on fear block our energy system, whereas positive thoughts based on love allow the energy to flow freely. Our emotions offer an indicator as to whether we are connected to our true selves or disconnected by doubts and fears from the ego personality. Keeping ourselves in balance through energy healing techniques, releases stress, calms our nervous system and boosts our immune system.

My mother's work as a healer inspired me to follow a similar path even though I was once told *"Your way is not the way of your mother."* I learned Reiki, an ancient energy healing technique that accesses universal life force energy to help release blocked energy in the body. Once attuned to receive Reiki, the energy flows through the hands which are placed on the body over the chakras at the base, sacral, solar plexus, heart, throat, brow and crown helping to dissolve blocked energy and restore the body to balance. I also learned Emotional Freedom Techniques (EFT), a system developed by Gary Craig which uses tapping with the fingers on certain points on the body to release blocked energy in the meridian energy system, in a similar way that needles are used in acupuncture. This is effective for releasing trapped emotions, negative thoughts and beliefs thereby reducing stress, calming the mind and the nervous system which boosts the immune system. These are simple and effective techniques that are easy to learn and offer a way to stay centred and in balance when our emotions get the better of us. Energy hygiene is as important as dental hygiene for keeping us in good health. I use Reiki and EFT daily to keep myself in balance and whenever I feel stressed, I stop what I am doing and spend a few minutes tapping and within minutes I feel calmer and more relaxed. It is important to acknowledge how we feel and not beat ourselves up with guilt as that only keeps them stuck. Emotions underlay our experience of being human and keeping them in balance is key to staying healthy. Suffice to say that EFT has supported me in writing *Pioneering Spirit* as I have been releasing the emotions that have come up during my writing journey and I am truly grateful to have a simple tool at my fingertips to help me stay calm and centred. I also use The Emotion Codes which were developed by Dr Bradley Nelson using muscle testing to identify trapped emotions and release them using a magnet. Energy healing is a powerful way to clear our energy systems and keep ourselves in balance. As our awareness expands to accept we have an incredible mind-body-spirit connection which holds the key to health and wellbeing, we can look forward to the day when integrated health care is part of our everyday reality.

As I come to the end of our story, I am reminded of my climb up Mount Uritorco. The path began slowly and easily, becoming harder and harder the higher I climbed in a similar way to the deeper I went into our story, which at times took me round in circles without a clear sense of direction. I reached the summit as I reach the end of our story and can look back and see how far I have come. Each step up the mountain represented each time I showed up at my computer never knowing what I was going to write, no more than I knew where the path was taking me up the mountain. I simply knew I had to be there and keep going. Uncovering the ancestral trail was like climbing down the mountain, more painful than climbing up as my body ached with sheer exhaustion. Emotionally, the responsibility of writing about my mother and my ancestors has been immense. Yet, the insights and realisations I have discovered about my life has led me to understand myself in ways I would never have known, had I not undertaken this journey. My ancestors started this trail generations ago, but it is thanks to my mother for asking me to write her story that I undertook the journey at all.

We become who we are when we identify with our personal story and see it as the reason why we are who we are. Yet, if we can detach from the dramas we have created, we can see it as simply a story. Ultimately, we need to let go of our story about Who We Think We Are because we cannot heal ourselves if we are attached to the identity created by the shadow, which hides Who We Truly Are. The journey I have been on through writing *Pioneering Spirit* has shown me that I need to let go of my story in order to recreate a new story for myself, one built on love and joy, rather than heartbreak and sadness. This experience has helped me understand myself in a new way and I am grateful to all those people who have guided me on my journey to wholeness. Ultimately we are all searching for the same, a place of love and safety where we feel at home, except we search outside of ourselves to find that place when the journey to wholeness is the inner journey into our self. It has taken me a lifetime to realise that home is where the heart is and healing the wound of separation is the journey we are all undertaking. May your journey unfold with love, ease and grace.

On a walk along the beach at West Wittering in the summer of 2012, the following words came into my mind

> *Look not back with regret*
> *For what's done is done*
> *Look to the future*
> *For the dreams that come*
> *Out of the ashes of yesterday*
> *To make way for a new tomorrow*
> *Let go of your pain*
> *The sadness and tears*
> *Replace them with joy*
> *In your beautiful heart*
> *The way may be uncertain*
> *And clouded with doubt*
> *Have faith and trust*
> *In the power of Love*

An Extraordinary Conscious Writing Journey

"An energy working for a higher purpose moved me to write this book"

I breathed a sigh of relief. Finally, *Pioneering Spirit* had reached a point of completion. I paused for a moment and reflected on the writing journey I had undertaken and realised what had evolved over the years as the book took shape, had been as important as completing the manuscript. It had been an unfolding journey of consciousness; living and writing; following my inner guidance and being led by my inner teacher. From the first moment I sat down to write, I had taken an adventure, which unfolded in ways I never imagined were possible and which were certainly beyond my human mind to control or understand. I realised through the transformational process of my writing, my understanding about myself had been revealed as the words flowed onto the page.

The journey began when my mother first asked me to write her life story. It is doubtful I would have agreed to her suggestion had I known how long it would take and with no idea about how I was going to accomplish it. Yet, the rewards I have gained in my willingness to be of service have been worth their weight in gold.

With the idea of writing a book in mind, I signed up for How To Write A Book Proposal Workshop at the Mind Body Spirit Show, in London, in 2007, facilitated by Julia McCutchen. Julia described the steps from book writing to publication which made it sound so simple. All I had to do was write the book! I began by making notes on the stories mum was telling me and drew up a timeline of her life, the surface physical context that gave her life meaning. However, I wanted to go deeper into understanding how she had achieved so much. What I didn't realise was that to find these answers about my mum, I needed to go deeper into myself.

Mum passed away in 2009 and it wasn't until 2013 that my creative doorway opened before me when Julia McCutchen offered me a place on her mentoring scholarship to work with her for six months through her International Association of Conscious and Creative Writers. I was invited to attend her Conscious Writing Workshop in London at the start of the programme. Our first exercise was to discover what our hearts truly wanted us to write about. Following her guidance, I connected to my heart and began to write, allowing the words to flow onto the page in my notebook without judgement. With my intention to write my mother's life story already decided, naturally this was what I expected to write about. But no, that day I discovered it was my story I really wanted to write, not my mother's. I finished writing and sat in shock and disbelief as my heart revealed its true calling. My mind immediately jumped in with thoughts of 'I have to do as I am told' filling me with guilt. I pondered on this revelation as deep down I knew my heart was telling me the truth even though my mind was doing its best to dissuade me. I left the workshop inspired and confused.

My first mentoring session with Julia followed a few days later and I told her what my heart had revealed. Julia encouraged me to put my mother's story to one side and focus on what my heart wanted to write. I followed her advice and the next day sat at my computer ready to begin. I stared at the blank page on the screen with no idea where to begin. I had given myself permission to write whatever I wanted except the choice was too immense. I took three conscious breaths and settled into my heart to allow space for my deeper creative self to take control. Yet again, I was in for a surprise because instead of beginning a factual account of my life's journey, an inspired story about a white horse began to unfold.

I finished writing the story and sat back in amazement. Where had that story come from? The way the tale unfolded surprised me as the ending showed me where to begin. I was being guided to connect with my childhood and allow the voice of my inner child to be heard. At the time I didn't realise I had been given insight into what was really going on in my heart, which only emerged when I began to write about my journey back in time.

I settled into my creative flow and wrote about my happy childhood in Argentina and how I loved the country where I was born and raised, and how it changed when we left and came to live in England. I allowed myself to connect with my inner child as she told me her story. I woke at 6am every morning and spent an hour, sometimes two hours, at the computer. I had an amazing feeling of riding a wave, inspired and energised. Julia kept me on track with our monthly chats and email check-ins, encouraging me to trust my creative spirit which was now in charge of my writing. I held nothing back as I unburdened years of sadness and kept thinking of *The White Horse* story I had written. Suddenly I realised my heart had revealed what I had buried long ago; the heartbreak of leaving the land I loved.

At the end of the six months' mentorship programme, I had completed the first draft of my story. I had no idea where to go next and the wave of inspiration I had felt was gone, replaced with mental, emotional and physical exhaustion. I started to read back what I had written and my mind, which had kept silent for so long, reminded me of my commitment to my mother. Perhaps I could integrate our stories together, after all, much of it we shared. I started to weave the two stories together, joining them like threads in a tapestry and began to note the similarities in our stories and the experiences we shared, which seem to have affected her parents, as well as my father and his parents. Clarity began to dawn. Mum had asked me to write about her life and to do that I needed to write about her parents and my father and how their parents went to Argentina which meant going into our ancestral story. It was there I discovered the pattern of migration of my ancestors which had been passed down the generations and which continued with my life of being born in one land and living my life in another. The answer to my question was being unveiled as I wrote. It was an inherited pattern passed down the ancestral lineage. It was then I knew I was no longer writing about myself and my mother but also our ancestral story.

I reflected on this sudden realisation and wondered if my ancestors had felt as I did when they left their homeland? Was this when the heartbreak had begun and if so, was there any way of releasing the deep emotional trauma it had left in our cellular memories? My mother's healing work had shown the potential of tapping into the subconscious mind and I am open to believing anything is possible. The answer came a few days later when I happened to listen to an Internet show called, Beyond The Ordinary, hosted by John Burgos interviewing Dr Bradley Nelson about Healing the Heart. Dr Nelson spoke about a system he created called The Emotion Code, described in his book *The Emotion Code,* which identifies trapped emotions in the body using muscle testing and releasing them using a magnet. It was similar to the way in which my mother had worked and even more interesting was to learn that it was possible to identify whether the emotions were inherited. I saw it as an answer to my prayer. I bought *The Emotion Code* and used The Emotion Code Chart to identify which of the emotions I was feeling were inherited and began to release my unconscious ancestral baggage.

My ancestral journey was taking me deeper into my inner healing and a workshop caught my attention at the Mind Body Spirit Show in Brighton called Healing the Family Tree. The facilitator was Natalia O'Sullivan, a holistic therapist and spiritual counsellor who had written a book co-authored with Nicola Graydon *The Ancestral Continuum, Unlock the secrets of who you really are.* The workshop offered insight into the emotions held within the chakras that guided me to book a personal session with Natalia to find out more about myself and my ancestral healing. In our session

Natalia took me to meet my ancestors and made me aware of the role I was playing in healing the family tree by writing my family story. I was surprised to learn it was something I had agreed to do.

With an understanding of the deeper picture, I continued to weave my mother's story and mine together as well as the ancestral story which was not easy. I persevered and booked a follow-up session with Julia who encouraged me to keep going. Eventually I completed Draft 2 of the manuscript and felt it was time for editorial feedback. I passed it to Jan Gavin, an editor I had been introduced to by my friend, Isabella. It was the first time anyone had read my work and I had no idea what feedback I would receive. Jan liked what I had written, but felt it would read better if I removed Mother's story. I couldn't believe it! All the hours I had spent putting the stories together was for nothing and I felt upset and deflated. Even so I had to admit Jan was right; my heart told me my mother's story and mine didn't fit together; we had to go our separate ways.

I felt I was going around in circles with no clear sense of direction. I took myself off for a few days to a spiritual retreat in Dorset to clear my head. I walked across the fields and had the same experience of going around in circles without finding my path! Life was showing me exactly what was going on in my confusion. However, six months later I completed Draft 3 and returned it to Jan, who said *"Much better!"* Thank goodness, except I had to work out how to present the story and that's when the idea came to split it three parts, My Ancestors, My Mother and Me.

In June 2016, I signed up for Julia's Conscious Writing Retreat in Glastonbury, a town I have visited many times, feeling a deep connection to this ancient part of England. I intended to be up at dawn to climb the Tor and anticipated a magic four days to unfold. Our first task was to complete a mind map of our current project. I did not feel inspired and wrote Choices in the circle on the page. From the circle I drew lines about what choices I had, mine, my mother's, my ancestor's, responsibility, emotions etc. The more lines I drew, the more lost and confused I became.

The depth of responsibility of my undertaking weighed heavily in my heart and the burden felt too much to bear. I collapsed in a heap of tears as I faced the reality of what I was doing and showed Julia my scrambled mind map. She looked at the paper, saw my distress and gently said, *"This is about your journey, Jeanine. As you heal yourself, you will heal your ancestors."*

The truth of what she said resonated deeply, it is where I had begun my conscious writing journey three years before when Julia encouraged me to write my story and not my mother's. I had become so focused on my mother and 'doing as I was told,' I had lost my way. Finally, I got the message, all I needed to do was to write my story as by writing my story, I was writing about my mother and my ancestors. The relief I felt was immense as my heart took charge again and let go of the confusion in my mind. I went for a walk to clear my head to process what had happened. The wind and the rain did not permit a climb to the Tor and I was exhausted and spent the rest of the day quietly in contemplation. The days unfolded but inspiration stayed out of reach and I never opened my computer. I felt depleted, in mind, body and spirit.

The last evening of the retreat gave us an opportunity to read our work to the group. I had nothing written that I wished to share and did not put my name down for this activity. But at the last moment I changed my mind because I saw a doorway was opening about being heard. I had brought with me a folder of the work I had submitted to Julia at the end of the mentoring programme and felt ready to share that with the group. When it was my turn, I began to read the Introduction and continued with *The White Horse* story. I felt emotions rising as I began to read and had to keep stopping to take a breath before continuing. It felt as though the voice of my inner child was being heard for the first time. I finished reading and returned to my chair with my heart pounding. At the end of the session, one of the group came up to me and said she had heard the voice of my inner child and felt intense emotion and extremely vulnerable, it was as though I had told her own story. The workshop ended and I felt a new part of me had emerged into the light.

I must have known I would need time to reintegrate to my usual lifestyle as I had booked to stay at the same spiritual place of refuge in Dorset, where I had been before. The house overlooks the sea and I knew I needed to walk along the beach among the ancient stones of the Jurassic coast, and allow the ocean to heal my heart. The next morning I set out as the rain continued to fall. I didn't care, it was where I needed to be. I returned from the beach, dried off and went to sit in a meditation hut in the garden of the retreat, with a magnificent view overlooking the bay. I took out my notebook and began to write. For the next four hours, as the rain kept falling, I kept writing as inspiration poured through me. My little writing sanctuary provided the perfect place to reconnect with my creative voice and let go of the emotion which had built up during the months of editing my manuscript. I was back in the flow of my heart, inspired and rejuvenated. I returned home and continued to write until I knew I had reached completion. I had fulfilled my mother's wish to write about her life and through the process I had been taken down a path to heal my heart and the ancestral timeline.

The journey to publication has been a long and winding road. A door opened to the Susan Mears Literary Agency where I was introduced to Wendy Yorke, a Book Editor and Author Coach and Literary Agent, who has been an inspiration in editing the manuscript and promoting my work at the International Book Fairs. Her support and belief in the message this book brings to a wider audience has guided me on my conscious writing journey and I am truly grateful she came into my life as my book angel.

TERMINOLOGY AND REFERENCES

Kinesiology Modalities

The Kinesiology Foundation (Correct at time of writing but please check website for updates) *www.kinesiologyfederation.co.uk*

- **Applied Kinesiology**
  Developed by American Chiropractor Dr George Goodheart. A system using muscle testing biofeedback to identify areas of imbalance in the meridian energy system in the body.

- **Health Kinesiology**
  Developed by American Psychologist, Dr Jimmy Scott PhD in the late 1970s.

  A system using muscle testing to rebalance the body and stimulate healing on physical, emotional, mental and spiritual levels.

- **Optimum Health Balance (OHB)**
  A kinesiology system developed by Charles Benham integrating a muscle response with the use of vibrational icons (visual symbols) that allow access to the deepest level of trauma or imbalance enabling blocked energy to be released and the cells to revert to their natural state of balance and the body restored to wellbeing.

- **One Brain**

  Also called, Three in One, integrates mind, body and spirit to release limiting thought patterns and creating new thoughts and behaviours based on what a person wishes to create for themselves.

- **Hyperton X**

  A technique developed by Frank Mahoney to release muscle tension and strengthen weak and painful muscles increasing movement and flexibility.

- **Kinergetics**

  An energy kinesiology method developed by Philip Rafferty
  www.kinergetics-reset.com

Touch For Health

Developed by Dr John Thie as a simplified version of Applied Kinesiology for anyone to use to maintain health and wellbeing without prior knowledge of the body and how it works.

Touch For Health Centre

www.touchforhealthcentre.co.uk

Aura-Soma

The Aura-Soma Colour Care system was developed by Vicky Wall in 1983 with her message, *"You are the colours you choose and the colours reflect your being's needs."* Bottles contain naturally extracted colours from flowers, plants and herbs, mixed with essential oils and the energy of crystals act as a mirror to our soul to help us see ourselves in a deeper way and restore balance on the physical, emotional, mental and spiritual levels of our human experience.

www.aura-soma.com

Chakra System

Chakra is a Sanskrit word meaning 'wheel of energy' through which vital life force energy flows into the body through nerve plexus and the endocrine system. The seven major chakras are traditionally associated with the colours of the rainbow and are located at the base (red), sacral (orange), solar plexus (yellow), heart (green), throat (blue), brow (indigo/royal blue) and crown (violet). There are also many minor chakras throughout the body creating an interlinking energy network system.

Crystal Healing

Crystal healing dates back to the Ancient Egyptians who used gems and crystals on and around the body to form an energy grid allowing their vibrations to balance the subtle energies. The colours of crystals are associated with the colours of the chakras.

Emotional Freedom Techniques

Founded by Gary Craig in 1995. A technique that integrates the Chinese meridian system by tapping on meridian end points on various parts of the body to release blocked emotional energy to reduce stress and calm the nervous system.
www.emofree.com

EmoTrance (Energy in Motion)

Developed by Silvia Hartmann based on her concept that stuck emotional energy can be released by focusing on the area in the body where the energy is felt and allowing the energy to soften and release.
www.dragonrising.com

Esoteric Healing (Subtle Energy Healing)

A specific approach to Spiritual Healing based on the understanding that life force energy needs to be able to flow freely into our minds and bodies for health and wellbeing. Subtle Energy Healing scans the energy field surrounding a person releasing any areas of imbalance, allowing the person's life force energy to flow freely once more and restoring their body to balance.

www.thehayloft-emsworth.org.uk
www.ineh.org.uk (International Network for Energy Healing)

Five Elements

China's elements of philosophy - Wood, Fire, Earth, Metal and Water connecting the meridian energy system of Chinese Acupuncture.

Matrix Reimprinting

Created by Emotional Freedom Technique Master, Karl Dawson in 2006, to transform the memory of a trauma or past event using a tapping sequence on different meridian end points on the face and hands to release stress and trauma associated with the event and the body rebalanced.

www.matrixreimprinting.com

Reiki

An ancient form of healing rediscovered by Dr Mikao Usui in Japan in the early 20th century using Universal Life Force energy (ki) to rebalance the body's subtle energy field by releasing stress and promoting healing and relaxation.

www.reikiassociation.net

Swedish Body Massage

A full body massage using long gliding strokes on the soft tissues of the body to release tension in the muscles, promoting relaxation and a feeling of wellbeing.

www.fht.org.uk/therapies/swedish-massage

The Emotion Codes

Developed by Dr Bradley Nelson, using applied kinesiology to identify and release trapped and inherited emotions with a magnet.

www.discoverhealing.com

The Radiance Technique (R trademark)

Developed by Dr Barbara Ray, a successor of Mrs Hawayo Takata, who studied Reiki under the lineage of Dr Mikao Usui.

www.trtia.org

RESOURCES

Andrea Garcia, Vibrational Therapist
www. andreagarcia.online

Conscious Writing for Creative Living
www.juliamccutchen.com

Museo O'Campo
La Cumbre, Argentina
Instagram or Facebook

5 Rhythms
www.5rhythms.com

Soul Motion (R trade mark)
www.sundacrisacredarts.com

Marisa Cheb Terrab Flow Dance
www.metodoflowdance.com.ar / www.marisachebterrab.com

Nick Poole, Chartered Psychologist,M.Ed, M.Sc., C. Psychol
www.nickpooleconsultation.co.uk

FURTHER READING

Booth Mike (2000) *Aura-Soma Handbook*, printed by Westermann Druck.

Brundell B (2005) *A Time Gone By, The Life and Work of the Leach Brothers* London: by Able Publishing 2005 (translation of the original published in Spanish Dr Sierra e Iglesias (1998) *Un Tiempo Que Se Fue.*

Coelho P (2005) *The Zahir.* London, HarperCollins Publishers.

Dawson K & Allenby S (2010) *Matrix Reimprinting using EFT, Rewrite your past, transform your future.* London, Hay House UK Ltd.

Goodwin D (2011) *Silver River.* London: Harper Perennial.

Holdway A (1995) *Kinesiology, Muscle Testing and Energy Balancing for Health and Well-Being.* Shaftesbury, Dorset United Kingdom, Element Books Limited.

Jones Richard (2005) *Mystical Britain and Ireland.* London, New Holland Publishers (UK) Ltd.

Lipton Dr B H (2005, 2011 - 10th anniversary edition) *The Biology of Belief: Unleashing the power of consciousness, matter and miracles.* New York, Hay House Inc.

Lynch V & P (2001) *Emotional Healing in Minutes, Simple acupressure techniques for your emotions.* London, Thorsons.

McCutchen Julia (2004) *The Writer's Journey from Inspiration to Publication.* Trowbridge, Firefly Media and (2015) *Conscious Writing, Discover your true voice through mindfulness and more.* London, Hay House UK Ltd.

Meunier Claudio, Garcia Carlos, Rimondi Oscar (2004) *Wings of Thunder.* (Also called *Alas de Trueno* in Spanish) published Buenos Aires, Argentina. Osvaldo Garraza Rosales, Bo "Manuel Lezcano", Mzna. M, Casa 13, San Luis.

Montefiore Santa (2001) *Meet Me Under the Ombu Tree* London, Simon & Schuster UK Ltd

and (2003) *The Forget-me-not Sonata.* London, Simon & Schuster UK Ltd.

Muir H J (1947) *Hoo Hooey* London, Country Life Ltd.

Nelson Dr Bradley (2007) *The Emotion Code, How to Release Your Trapped Emotions for Abundant Health, Love and Happiness.* Mesquite Nevada USA, Wellness Unmasked Publishing.

Nelson Dr Bradley (2019) *The Emotion Code Updated and Expanded.* Vemillion Penguin Random House UK.

O'Sullivan N & Graydon N (2013) *The Ancestral Continuum, Unlock the Secrets to Who You Really Are.* London, Simon & Schuster UK Ltd.

Pert C B (1998) *Molecules of Emotion, Why you feel the way you feel.* London, Simon & Schuster UK Ltd.

Thie Dr J F (1973, revised edition 1979) *Touch For Health, a practical guide to natural health using acupuncture touch and massage to improve postural balance and reduce physical and mental pain and tension.* Marina del Rey, CA, USA.

Wall V (2005) *Aura-Soma, Self-Discovery through Colour.* Vermont Healing Arts Press

Originally published in the United Kingdom in 1991 by Thorsons as *The Miracle of Colour Healing.*

Wilkinson S (1998) *Sebastian's Pride.* London, Michael Joseph Ltd.

ABOUT THE AUTHOR

Jeanine Brownrigg was born in Buenos Aires, Argentina, second generation Anglo-Argentine, of British parents. At 10 years of age, she returned with her family to live in England, where she now resides. Writing has been part of her life since her childhood and her career in the National Health Service, in a clerical and managerial role. Now retired, she focuses on her healing practice and writing career and also writes children's stories.

Jeanine is a trained and registered complementary therapy practitioner in Swedish Body and Indian Head Massage, the Aura-Soma Colour Care System, Reiki, Emotional Freedom Technique, EmoTrance (Energy in Motion) and Matrix Reimprinting and has a regular client practice.

Jeanine is a mother, grandmother and step-grandmother and lives with her husband in West Sussex. She enjoys theatre and dance, walking, yoga, reading and silk painting. Apart from Argentina, she has also travelled to countries in Europe, Central and South America and the Far East, and speaks fluent Spanish.

www.jeaninebrownrigg.co.uk